Racism and Sexism in Children's Books

GW01003496

Writers and Readers

Writers and Readers Publishing Cooperative
9-19 Rupert Street
London W1V 7FS, England 1979

Designed by Carole Driver

Typeset by Humble Wordsmith, Tonbridge

Printed by J.W. Arrowsmith Ltd, Bristol

Bound by The Camelot Press Ltd, Southampton

Contents

Acknowledgements

We would like to thank the Council on Interracial Books for Children for permission to reprint all the articles in this book with the exception of the following: "Enid Blyton's Girls" an extract from *You're A Brick, Angela!* by Mary Cadogan and Patricia Craig, for which we would like to thank Victor Gollancz Ltd.; "Oh! Please Mr. Tiger" for which we gratefully acknowledge the permission of the *Times Literary Supplement:* and "Uncle, Buy Me a Contraceptive", an extract from *How to Read Donald Duck: Imperialist Ideology in the Disney Comic* by Ariel Dorfman and Armand Mattelart, translated and introduced by David Kunzle, reprinted by permission of International General Editions, Inc., New York.

Introduction

This is a new and updated version of the book first published in Britain by Writers and Readers in 1976. Far more essays have now been included as the debate about racism and sexism in literature continues, and more material becomes available.

Our shops and libraries contain so many different children's books, both fiction and non-fiction, that it is difficult to make a choice. There are so many pitfalls. Readers may feel that considerations of style, clarity, the quality of the illustrations, the size of the print (and, in some cases, the price of the book) are problems enough. Why create more?

Children are very much influenced by the books they read, particularly at a younger level. Many of the books they come across will be old ones with outdated ideas where sugar is something that little girls are made of, and harvested by smiling black natives. We are now living in a multi-racial society, and one where women are determined to achieve real equality. Our literature, and especially our children's literature, should reflect these preoccupations. To help readers in their choice, various well-known and often widely-accepted stories are examined in these essays for their attitudes to race and sex, while further aid is offered by the guidelines at the end of the book.

Even now books are still being produced which are tainted by the old colonialist assumptions. *The Cay* is a case in point. Like *Robinson Crusoe,* it is an adventure story whose main interest lies in the struggle for survival on a desert island. Both books reinforce racist attitudes, *Crusoe* with its treatment of cannibalism and the dog-like Friday, *The Cay* with its portrayal of Timothy, the subservient West Indian who saves the hero's life. While we cannot expect *Robinson Crusoe* to show many mid-twentieth century attitudes, there is no such excuse for *The Cay*. (As for Defoe's novel, an end to abridgements of such 'classics' would mean that children would be unlikely to read the novel until they were old enough to judge it for themselves.)

The Slave Dancer is more interesting and more complex than *The Cay*. The interdependence of slave and slaver — and the degradation the traffic brings to both — is convincingly shown through the young boy Jessie (whose outburst of hatred against the slaves is surely intended to show just how low he has been brought). Unfortunately, as Lyla Hoffman's essay makes clear, it is still almost exclusively a white view of the subject. This raises the question of whether it is a topic best left to black writers for the moment. The slaves are depicted as a passive mass, with only the young boy Ras at all developed as a character.

Black people are often anonymous figures in children's literature. Timothy in *The Cay* is lucky enough to be given a first name. None of the characters in *Sounder* has a name at all (apart from the dog!). This is obviously a conscious literary device to bring universality to the story: even so it's an ill-chosen one.

This doesn't mean, though, that white writers should never try to describe the black experience, only that they should 'confront their own racism' in writing. As John Rowe Townsend has pointed out in *Written for Children* (Kestrel 1974), if writers only described things they themselves had experienced, there would be no room for creative imagination — and no stories about the past at all!

There have been many well-meaning attempts, mainly by white writers, to show that black and white are the same 'under the skin'. But there *are* differences, just as there are differences between the sexes (which are derided or denied in the *Pippi Longstocking* series). These differences should be valued, not ignored or dismissed. People should be accepted for what they are, and have to offer — and not be judged by preconceptions.

Stereotyped attitudes can disfigure what otherwise might be charming or useful books. Prince Bumpo, the African who appears in several of the *Dr Dolittle* series, is inferior (except in strength) even to the Doctor's parrot. His appearance and way of speaking are equally ridiculous. Curiously, Hugh Lofting, the author of the books, once remarked that all races were about equal morally. But this view does not emerge from his stories — which is a pity, for some of his other concerns, such as conservation (tigers shouldn't be kept in zoos, the North Pole should be left to polar bears) are strikingly modern.

It would be wasteful to cast off these books entirely. Judicious cutting when reading aloud, or an avoidance of the titles which feature Bumpo, would mean we could still keep the good things that Lofting has to offer. (The *Mary Poppins* series by P.L. Travers could also be treated in this way.) Better still, a parent or teacher could use these more dubious aspects as material for discussion of the whole problem.

There are, of course, dangers in examining children's books for their racist or sexist attitudes alone. The main one is that, in the process, we could lose more than we gain.

A case in point is fairy tales. At a superficial glance, these could be regarded as both sexist (all those beautiful maidens) and elitist (they're princesses as well!). They could only be considered racist by omission. But fairy tales are not realistic, except in the occasional detail, and are hardly ever taken as such even by the smallest child. They are not intended to work at this level. As Bruno Bettelheim has shown in *The Uses of Enchantment* (Thames and Hudson, 1976) children can learn from these age-old tales about the inner problems of human beings and how they can be faced or solved. (The tales are of great antiquity. The story we know as Cinderella is based on one found written down in China around 850 A.D.).

In other areas, though, there is no need to tread so carefully. Any school reader in which the sex-roles are spelt out (the older brother climbs a tree, the little sister admires from below) should be scrapped. These are purpose-built books which house harmful attitudes, like those history and geography textbooks still bristling with colonialist assumptions. And the same applies to dictionaries (try looking up doctor, or doll, or domestic) and sex education books. These are strictly works of reference, and the references should fit today's needs.

The parent, the teacher, the writer and the reader can hope to avoid only some of these pitfalls. It would be virtually impossible, for instance, to stop a child coming into contact with *Charlie and the Chocolate Factory,* a book notable both for its great popularity and its general lack of humanity. If a child has been taught consideration for others and to question the value of what she reads, then the problem will be diminished accordingly.

Most of this selection of essays came originally from the *Interracial Digest* Nos 1 & 2, first published by the Council for Interracial Books for Children in the United States. The majority of the books under discussion can be found in this country. (English editions are given where available, and quotations are taken wherever possible from the paperback edition.)

The chapters on Puerto Rican and Chicano books have been omitted from this new edition. Although not available here, these books do have lessons for the English reader. For instance, in Puerto Rican books, the minority-group child is repeatedly shown as living in a ghetto. The continual suggestion that this is the norm must surely help to make it so, when really these conditions are inherited rather than inherent. Women are shown as even more passive than in standard literature. No attempt is made to give children pride in their race. They are too often saved by the intervention of a white person. And inattention to detail (Italian names, say, instead of Spanish ones) reveal the basic lack of concern.

Almost all of the books mentioned in the essay on Children's Books and the Black Identity are not available here either. American writers are well ahead of their British counterparts in this area, and we can benefit from their experience. Another new direction is shown by the Chinese in their books where children are seriously treated as potential adults.

It is hoped that both these essays and the guidelines will encourage a new approach to the writing and criticism of children's literature.

Judith Stinton
London 1979.

Racism in Children's Books

From Caricature to Character

Attitudes to Race as shown through illustration

" Let me go, you savage!"

Mary Poppins series:
P.L. Travers and
Mary Shepard

Sounder:
William H Armstrong and James Barkley

Sean's Red Bike:
Petronella Breinburg and Errol Lloyd

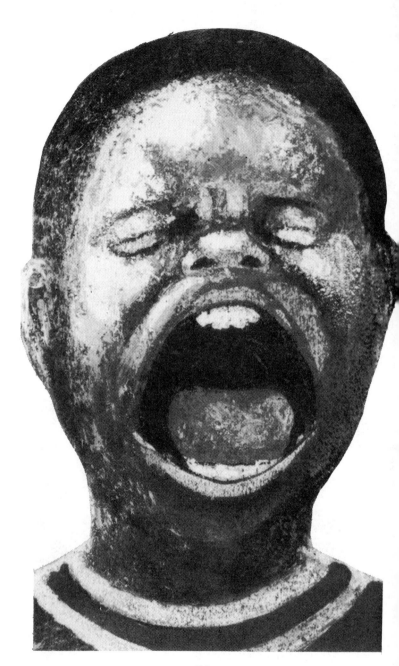

My Brother Sean
Petronella Breinburg &
Errol Lloyd

*Dr Dolittle's Post
Office:*
Hugh Lofting

Huckleberry Finn:
Mark Twain and C. Walter Hodges

'Doan' hurt me—don't!'

Little Black Sambo:
Helen Bannerman

Left — Uncle Tom's Cabin:
Harriet Beecher Stowe

Charlie and the Chocolate ›
Factory:
Roald Dahl and Faith Jaques

Pet Show!:
Ezra Jack Keats

Men of the Road:
Charles King

crystal
ball

Gypsies and Nomads:
Ruth Thomson and
Peter Connolly

Five Chinese Brothers:
Claire Huchet Bishop
and Kurt Wiese

Doctor Dolittle —
The Great White Father

Isabelle Suhl

The article below was the Council on Interracial Books' first major revaluation of a children's classic for its racist content, and it started a chain reaction. News stories appeared first in The New York Times *and then in other papers across the U.S. Editorials debated its pros and cons. And the London* Times, *considering the whole question to be heretical, dismissed the review as simply an unwarranted and malicious attack on a beloved English author.*

Several years have passed. Recently, the original publishers told the Council that they were planning to discontinue active promotion of the Doctor Dolittle books. Few recommended booklists still feature the series. It would seem that the reading public is becoming more selective, and that publishers for the first time are feeling the squeeze.

Who is the "real" Doctor Dolittle? And what manner of man was his creator, Hugh Lofting, who for more than fifty years has been hailed as a genius and his books as "classics" by teachers, librarians and children's book reviewers? Rarely has a word of criticism of him or his books been heard.

After carefully examining four of the most popular books *(The Story of Doctor Dolittle, The Voyages of Doctor Dolittle, Doctor Dolittle's Post Office* and *Doctor Dolittle's Zoo),* I charge that the "real" Doctor Dolittle is the personification of the Great White Father Nobly Bearing the White Man's Burden and that his creator was a white racist and chauvinist, guilty of almost every prejudice known to modern white Western man, especially an Englishman growing up in the last years of the Victorian age, when the British

Empire was at its zenith.* These attitudes permeate the books
I read and are reflected in the plots and actions of the stories,
in the characterisations of both animals and people as well as
in the dialogue.

Consider the situation in *The Voyages of Doctor Dolittle,*
the second of the books published (1922) and winner of the
1923 Newbery Medal as "the most distinguished contribution
to children's literature" in that year. Doctor Dolittle,
accompanied by Prince Bumpo, ten-year-old Tommy
Stubbins, Polynesia the parrot, Chee-Chee the monkey and
Jip the dog, arrives on Spidermonkey Island off the coast of
Brazil in search of the "Red Indian" Long Arrow, the
world's greatest naturalist. On his first day on the island,
Doctor Dolittle rescues Long Arrow and a group of Indians
entombed in a cave and brings fire to the heretofore fireless
Indians of Popsipetel. This makes him so popular that he is
constantly followed about by crowds of admirers. "After his
fire-making feat, this childlike people expected him, I think,
to be continually doing magic." He solves problem after
problem for the Indians and eventually they ask the "Mighty
One" to become "the King of the whole Spidermonkey
Island."

Reluctantly he accepts and, as King Jong, becomes, of
course, the hardest-working, most democratic king in all
history. He brings his new subjects many of the blessings of
white civilisation — proper sewerage, rubbish collection, a
pure water-supply system, etc. He locates iron and copper
mines and shows the Indians how to use metal. He holds
court in the morning to settle all kinds of disputes, teaches
thousands in the afternoon and visits the sick in the evening.
After a while, though, he wants to go home. He realises that
"these people have come to rely on me for a great number of
things. We found them ignorant of much that white people

* It should be noted that Hugh Lofting, though brought up in
England, spent most of his adult life in the U.S. His first
book, *The Story of Doctor Dolittle,* was published in the U.S.
in 1920, two years before it appeared in England.

enjoy. And we have, one might say, changed the current of their lives considerably... I cannot close my eyes to what might happen if I should leave these people and run away. They would probably go back to their old habits and customs: wars, superstitions, devil-worship and what not; and many of the new things we have taught them might be put to improper use and make their condition, then, worse by far than that in which we found them... They are, as it were my children... I've got to stay."

His animal friends have different ideas. Polynesia the parrot "had grown very tired of the Indians and she made no secret of it. 'The very idea,' she said... 'the idea of the famous John Dolittle spending his valuable life waiting on these greasy natives! — Why, it's preposterous!'" In a few days Polynesia works out all the details of their departure, comes up with all the answers to the Doctor's objections and even succeeds in getting Long Arrow to urge the Doctor to leave. With that the Doctor gives in. Laying his crown on the beach where his "poor children" will find it and know he has gone, he heads back for England to carry on his "proper work" — taking care of the animals of the world.

This adventure with the Indians was not the Doctor's first experience at playing the Great White Father to ignorant natives. In *Doctor Dolittle's Post Office,* he had served a somewhat similar function for the West African kingdom of Fantippo. This book was the third one published (1923), but the events take place between *The Story of Doctor Dolittle* and *The Voyages.* In this story he is not actually made king, but as the end of the book neatly summarises:

People who have written the history of the Kingdom of Fantippo all devote several chapters to a mysterious white man who in a very short space of time made enormous improvements in the mail, the communications, the shipping, the commerce, the education and the general prosperity of the country. Indeed, it was through John Dolittle's quiet influence that King Koko's reign came to be looked upon as the Golden Age in Fantippan history. A wooden statue still stands in the market-place to his memory.

In contrast, the pre-Dolittle years of King Koko's reign were not so "golden". In those days he occasionally made war on other African tribes and took many prisoners. Some he sold as slaves to white traders if they offered him especially high prices; others he kept for himself "because he liked to have strong men at his court". He greatly admired the ways of the "civilised world" and tried to copy and compete with it. That was how he had come to set up a post office in the first place, a most unusual thing to find "in a savage African kingdom". After many false starts, he got it functioning, until one day a "white man explained to him this new craze for stamp collecting that was sweeping over the civilised world". He immediately shifted from selling stamps for mailing purposes to selling stamps for stamp collections. It was a profitable business for his kingdom, but "the Fantippo mail service was neglected and became very bad". He then had to invite Doctor Dolittle to come to Fantippo and "arrange the post office for him and put it in order so it would work properly".

The King is depicted, both in text and drawings, as a ludicrous figure. A very vain man, he always insisted — before, during and after the Doctor's sojourn in Fantippo — that the stamps for the post office "must all have my beautiful face upon them, and no other". He was usually found "sitting at the palace door, sucking a lollipop — for he, like all Fantippos, was very fond of sweetmeats". When he wasn't sucking one, he used it as a "quizzing glass" to peer through in the "elegant manner" of white men. "But constant lollipops had ruined his figure and made him dreadfully stout. However, as fatness was considered a sign of greatness in Fantippo, he didn't mind that." When Doctor Dolittle was ready to inaugurate his foreign mail service, it was King Koko who brought the first letter to be sent off by the Swallow Mail. And to whom did he send it? A friend of his "who runs a shoe-shine parlour in Alabama"!

All the other African characters in this book are depicted in like manner as quaint, comic, and childlike, with simple minds, ridiculous customs and funny-sounding names. Even the animals can feel superior to them.

In *The Voyages,* Chee-Chee the monkey recounts how he escaped from Africa by disguising himself in clothes stolen from "a fashionable black lady". The idea had come to him when he saw "a lot of people, black and white, getting on a ship that was coming to England". One of the children of a "big family of funny people" reminded him of a cousin of his. "'That girl,' he said to himself, 'looks just as much like a monkey as I look like a girl.'"

The most famous of all Lofting's African characters is Prince Bumpo. He is at the same time his most outrageous creation, but apparently he was dear to the author's heart because he is one of the few human characters to appear in several books. He first appeared in *The Story of Doctor Dolittle* and reappears as a major character in *The Voyages* and as a minor one in *Doctor Dolittle's Zoo.*

It is in *The Story of Doctor Dolittle* that Prince Bumpo becomes white. Doctor Dolittle and his animal friends, homeward-bound after curing the sick monkeys of Africa, are captured for the second time by the King of the Jolliginki, Prince Bumpo's father. Polynesia the parrot slips out of prison, sees Bumpo in the garden reading fairy tales and overhears him say, "If I were only a *white* prince!" She tells Bumpo that a famous wizard, John Dolittle, is in his father's prison. "Go to him, brave Bumpo, secretly... and behold, thou shalt be made the whitest prince that ever won fair lady!" Then she rushes back to the Doctor and convinces him that if they are to succeed in escaping prison he must fulfill her promise, no matter what tricks are necessary to do it. Bumpo arrives as planned and begs the Doctor to turn him white so that he can return to The Sleeping Beauty who spurned him because he was black. The Doctor concocts a mixture of liquids which turns the Prince's face white. In gratitude, Prince Bumpo lets them out of prison and gives them a ship in which to sail away.

23

This summary merely suggests the objectionable nature of the episode, where every line is replete with insults and ridicule. It is impossible for Lofting to depict Africans, be they kings, princes or ordinary people, with dignity and genuine human qualities. To him they are only vehicles for so-called humour.

But even more than that, as one black critic put it, Bumpo can find no happiness in his blackness, and is "willing to sell out everything — even his father's authority — to 'become white,'" which in any event he cannot remain.

If the characterisation of Bumpo in *The Story of Doctor Dolittle* is bad, it is worse in *The Voyages.* Even defenders of Hugh Lofting have had to denounce the racism of the white prince episode, but I have yet to see or hear any serious criticism of *The Voyages.* This book is, apparently, sacrosanct because it is a Newbery Award winner.

Early in *The Voyages,* Polynesia the parrot returns to Doctor Dolittle's household after five years in Africa. One of the Doctor's first questions concerns Bumpo. Polynesia informs him that Bumpo is now in England, studying at Oxford University. The Doctor is naturally surprised. Polynesia adds, "He was scared to death to come... He thought he was going to be eaten by white cannibals or something. You know what those niggers are — that ignorant!"

When the Doctor asks whether Bumpo ever found The Sleeping Beauty, Polynesia replies:

"'Well, he brought back something which he *said* was The Sleeping Beauty. Myself, I think it was an albino nigeress...'

'And tell me, did he remain white?'

'Only for about three months,' said the parrot. '... It was just as well. He was so conspicuous in his bathing-suit the way he was, with his face white and the rest of him black.'"

On the many occasions in all the books where they are together, Polynesia always speaks insultingly of and to Bumpo. Never once does the "good, kind" Doctor object or reprove her for her bad manners, to say nothing of her degrading attitude.

Shortly after this, the Doctor decides to go on the voyage to Spidermonkey Island, described earlier. He is looking for a third crewman, when there appears "a most extraordinary-looking black man". He "was dressed in a fashionable frock coat with an enormous bright red cravat. On his head was a straw hat with a gay band; and over this he held a large green umbrella. He was very smart in every respect except his feet. He wore no shoes or socks." Who is this apparition of sartorial splendour? Why, of course, none other than "Bumpo Kahbooboo, Crown Prince of Jolliginki"! (In both name and attire, does he not call to mind that other "classic", *Little Black Sambo?*) To the solicitous Doctor, Bumpo explains his "absconsion" from the University as temporary, adding that his education will not be neglected on board ship anyway, the Doctor being of "great studiosity".

From this point on, both in *The Voyages* and *Doctor Dolittle's Zoo*, Bumpo speaks mainly in malapropisms — once more, the ridiculous African trying unsuccessfully to be white, this time by imitating the speech pattern of a cultured, educated Englishman.

At first glance the interracial nature of the crew might be construed as a positive contribution to race relations, but not in these books. Once underway, Bumpo, African prince and Oxford scholar, is consigned to the stereotyped role of cook for the rest of the crew.

In his characterisation of Bumpo, Lofting has missed few of the colonial Englishman's views of the "savage" nature of Africans. In tense, dangerous situations Bumpo is seen as a man of loyalty and great brawn, little brain and brute violence. On several occasions in different books, he shows himself ready at the drop of a hat to resort to murder to save his friends. But even Polynesia the parrot knows better, and they stop him in the nick of time. As Polynesia reminds him when he proposes killing the stowaway who has been eating up the ship's store of salt beef, "No. We'd get into trouble. We're not in Jolliginki now, you know — worse luck!" Or, as Doctor Dolittle tells him when he proposes eliminating the "useless" Throgmorton in *Doctor Dolittle's Zoo*, "You're not in Africa now, Bumpo. Put him down..." There is even one suggestion of cannibalism as a solution to a problem. Polynesia worries that they have no money with which to replace the salt beef the stowaway ate. "'Would it not be good political economy,' Bumpo whispered back, 'if we salted the able seaman and ate him instead?'" Polynesia again reminds him that they are not in Jolliginki, and besides, "those things are not done on white men's ships."

Extravagant praise has been heaped on Lofting's illustrations. Many are, indeed, delightful, but all the drawings of Africans are as insulting and offensive as the text — grotesque caricatures.

Several publishers issued new Dolittle books to tie in with the release of the Doctor Dolittle movie in 1968. I wish to comment on only one, Cape's *Doctor Dolittle: A Treasury.* The publisher's foreword describes their pride in being the publisher of the Dolittle books and asserts that the material in the *Treasury* is *"just as Hugh Lofting wrote it".* This is not exactly truthful. The book contains excerpts from eight of the twelve Dolittle titles and was very carefully edited by Olga Fricker, sister of the late Mrs. Hugh Lofting. Nowhere in any of the selections does Bumpo appear, although his distorted portrait is in the reproduction of the original title page of *The Story of Doctor Dolittle,* which is included. That whole book has been reduced to fifteen pages. The largest excerpt is from *The Voyages* (116 pages), but no longer is there a "third man" in the crew. Bumpo's original role has been assigned to one or another of the characters, animal or human. Olga Fricker seems to understand better than her publisher that it is no longer possible to publish a Lofting story "just as he wrote it".

Mary Poppins Revised: An Interview with P.L. Travers

Albert V. Schwartz

Did you know that there is a new version of *Mary Poppins?*
This popular piece of children's literature, once described by
the *Christian Science Monitor* as "whimsical, philosophic, and
strong in the principles of good thinking", has been revised so
as to mitigate its racism.

When I first made this discovery, I phoned the children's
department of the American publisher, Harcourt Brace
Jovanovich, to find out how these changes had come about. I
was told that certain portions of the original text had been
revised in the 1972 paperback edition at the request of the
author.

What had caused the author to make these changes? The
editor said she did not know but she put me in touch with
P.L. Travers herself, who is living in New York. I promptly
called her and was delighted to hear that she was willing to
grant me an interview.

I met Ms. Travers in her apartment on a rainy day. How
appropriate to be arriving with an umbrella in my hand and
wellingtons on my feet! When we sat in her living room, I
found I was face to face with the stern, bright, sharp "Mary"
of my readings.

We talked for a long time before Ms. Travers would let me
begin taping the discussion. She interviewed me almost as
much as I her. I told her that the Council on Interracial
Books for Children had been receiving more and more
complaints about her stereotyped presentation of Africans,
Chinese, Eskimos, and American Indians in *Mary Poppins,*
most particularly in the chapter "Bad Tuesday".

Sitting tall and tense, Pamela Travers was aware of every word as she spoke: "Remember, *Mary Poppins* was written a long time ago [1934] when racism was not as important. About two years ago, a schoolteacher friend of mine, who is a devotee of *Mary Poppins* and reads it constantly to her class, told me that when she came to that part [i.e., the trip to Africa in "Bad Tuesday";] it always made her shudder and squirm if she had black children in her class. I decided that if that should happen, if even one black child were troubled, or even if *she* were troubled, then I would have to alter it. And so I altered the conversation part of it. I didn't alter the plot of the story. When the next edition, which was the paperback, came out, I also altered one or two things which had nothing to do with 'piccaninny' talk at all.

"Various friends of mine, artists and writers, said to me, 'No, no! What you have written you have written. Stand by it!' But, I thought, no, if the least of these little ones is going to be hurt, I am going to alter it!"

Ms. Travers told me that she didn't know where she had picked up the "piccaninny" language since, she said, she had known no black people at the time she wrote *Mary Poppins*. However, she had read *Uncle Remus* and still knows *Little Black Sambo* by heart.

I said that it was fortunate that she had also eliminated the references to watermelon and shoe polish. But when I asked why she herself still used the term "piccaninny", she replied: "To me, even now the word 'piccaninny' is very pretty. I've used it myself time and time again to children. Not to black children because life hasn't brought me very much in contact with black children, but I've used it time and again to small children."

When asked what language the black characters used in the revised version, Ms. Travers said: "Formal English, grave and formal. Now that I've met black people from time to time, they speak a formal English."

Many of my comments about other parts of *Mary Poppins* displeased Ms. Travers. "I refuse to be arraigned for what I wrote," she declared at one point. "You're overstressing from

28

the point of view of racism, which is something I don't
accept. I have no racism in me. I wasn't born with it. And it's
never happened inside of me. And therefore I feel perfectly at
ease and at home no matter what colour anybody's skin is. I
was brought up in a family and in a world where there was no
hint of racism of any kind. And not because my family was
liberal or because they had liberal friends. I was brought up
by large-minded people who never had any sense of racism at
all. I grew up in a rarefied atmosphere. I loved *Little Black
Sambo* as a child... I only came across racism when I came to
the United States.''

"If you grew up without racism, with parents who had no
racism, then how do you explain that racism appears in your
books?'' I asked.

"Literature and imagination are my world. I don't like
being pulled out of that world and being forced to live in a
sociological world of which I am not a native inhabitant.
Imagination is a pure thing. It is envisaging. Imagination does
not depend upon the sociology of the time. More functional
books do; imagination does not. Imagination goes whither it
will. *Mary Poppins* is not a contemporary book. It is a
timeless book, and probably it goes back a good deal to my
own childhood.

"I am not really convinced that any harm is done,'' she
continued. ''I remember when I was first invited to New York
by a group of schoolteachers and librarians, amongst whom
were many black teachers. We met at the New York Public
Library. I had thought that they expected me to talk to them,
but no, on the contrary, they wanted to thank me for writing
Mary Poppins because it had been so popular with their
classes. Not one of them took the opportunity — if indeed
they noticed it — to talk to me about what you've mentioned
in 'Bad Tuesday'.''

Another question I had for P.L. Travers regarded the
insulting use of the term "street arab". Miss Lark, a
character in *Mary Poppins*, calls to her dog to get away from
the other dogs: "Andrew, Andrew, come in, my darling!
Come away from those dreadful street arabs!''

Pamela Travers laughed at the question. "Is that a pejorative term? 'Street arab'? There are 'street arabs' in Morocco, aren't there? Little boys running around asking for hashish? Are you trying to arraign me for that? Because I shan't be in any way arraigned or put in a witness box. I used it! Very well, then. That's what it meant to me at the time, and there it is. I never thought of changing it. If anybody said it made them squirm I would have changed that too. But I don't think that any normal person would squirm at that term."

Pamela Travers agreed that Mary Shepard's illustrations for the chapter, "Bad Tuesday" were stereotypes but said that she was not responsible for them. (The editors at Harcourt Brace Jovanovich later said that when revisions of the book were considered, at no time was any thought given to changing Mary Shepard's illustrations, which often show stereotyped Third World people.)

The original passage from the chapter "Bad Tuesday" — still in the hardcover edition generally found in schools and libraries — is as follows:

Beneath the palm-tree sat a man and a woman, both quite black all over and with very few clothes on. But to make up for this they wore a great many beads — some hung around their heads just below great crowns of feathers, some in their ears, one or two in their noses. Beads were looped about their necks and plaited bead belts surrounded their waists. On the knee of the negro lady sat a tiny black piccaninny with nothing on at all. It smiled at the children as its Mother spoke.

"Ah bin 'specting you a long time, Mar' Poppins," she said, smiling. "You bring dem chillun dere into ma li'l house for a slice of watermelon right now. My, but dem's very white babies. You wan' to use a li'l bit black boot polish on dem. Come 'long, now. You'se mighty welcome."

And she laughed, loud happy laughter, as she got up and began to lead the way towards a little hut made entirely of palm-trees.

Jane and Michael were about to follow, but Mary Poppins held them back.

"We've no time to stay, unfortunately. Just dropped in as we were passing, you know. We've got to get round the world —" she explained to the two black people who lifted up their hands in surprise.

"You got some journey, Mar' Poppins," said the man.

In the paperback edition this passage reads as follows:

"We've been anticipating your visit, Mary Poppins," she said, smiling. "Goodness, those are very pale children! Where did you find them? On the moon?" She laughed at them, loud happy laughter, as she got to her feet and began to lead the way to a little hut made of palm-leaves. "Come in, come in and share our dinner. You're all as welcome as sunlight."

However, the description of the black parents is still grotesque stereotyping; and the image of the mother's childish simplicity is unchanged: "She laughed again as if this, and everything else in the world, were one huge happy joke."

Nor have other racist elements in "Bad Tuesday" been touched. Two of the four visits (to the North and to the East) are just long enough for Mary Poppins to be recognised and welcomed — and for the briefest stereotyped image of an Eskimo and a Chinese Mandarin to register on the reader's imagination. In the fourth visit, to the American West, an encounter takes place — or at least begins to take place. Michael, the little white boy, is challenged by Chief Sun-at-Noonday, to "try his strength against my great-great-great-grandson, Fleet-as-the-Wind!" Fleet-as-the-Wind easily outruns the two visiting children, but "Michael was angry now and set his teeth and fled screaming after Fleet-as-the-Wind, determined not to be outrun by an Indian boy." Michael, who is probably not more than seven years old, automatically assumes the "white man's burden" and has to

31

prove his superiority to "an Indian boy". However, Mary
Poppins interrupts the chase by whisking the children back to
their own home.

The final scene of "Bad Tuesday" begins when Michael
secretly takes the magic compass for his own use.

A noise behind the chair startled him and he turned
round guiltily, expecting to see Mary Poppins. But instead,
there were four gigantic figures bearing down towards him
— the Eskimo with a spear, the Negro Lady with her
husband's huge club, the Mandarin with a great curved
sword, and the Red Indian with a tomahawk. They were
rushing upon him from all four quarters of the room with
their weapons raised above their heads, and, instead of
looking kind and friendly as they had done that afternoon,
they now seemed threatening and full of revenge. They
were almost on top of him, their huge, terrible, angry faces
looming nearer and nearer. He felt their hot breath on his
face and saw their weapons tremble in their hands.

With a cry Michael dropped the compass.

"Mary Poppins, Mary Poppins — help me, help me!" he
screamed, and shut his eyes tight.

This racist nightmare in which Third World people turn —
without the slightest provocation — into monsters to punish a
white child remains unaltered in the new version of *Mary
Poppins*. Viewed as the product of a cultural fantasy, as an
expression of racist fears of retribution, this scene may make
perfect sense; but if this view is accepted or not, it is clearly
irresponsible to teach children to identify their fears of
punishment with Third World people.

A closer look at three of the Mary Poppins books — *Mary
Poppins* (1934), *Mary Poppins Comes Back* (1935), and *Mary
Poppins in the Park* (1952) — shows that Mary Poppins and
other adults in the stories consistently use non-white peoples
to symbolise "improper" or "wrong" behaviour.

From *Mary Poppins* (page 185): Michael's mother says:

"You will *not* behave like a Red Indian, Michael."

From *Mary Poppins Comes Back* (page 61) Mary Poppins: "Not one step will you go out of this room this afternoon, or I'm a Chinaman." (Page 115) "Then they became Red Indians with John and Barbara for squaws." (Page 133) "Walk beside me, please, like a Christian." (Page 181) Mary Poppins: "I would rather," she remarked with a sniff, "have a family of Cannibals to look after. They'd be more human!" (Page 185) Mary Poppins: "A *Zulu* would have better manners!"

From *Mary Poppins in the Park:* (page 61) Mary Poppins to the grimy children: "You look like a couple of Blackamoors!" (Page 128) Mary Poppins: "May I ask what you think you're doing, Jane? And you, too, Michael! Let go that Policeman! Is this a garden or a Cannibal Island?" (Page 142) Mary Poppins to an upset and excited Michael: "I understand that you're behaving like a Hottentot." (Page 185) Mary Poppins with a disapproving look at the children: "A pair of Golliwogs — that's what you are!"

From *Friend Monkey* (a recent book, published in 1971) page 61: Stanley Livingstone Fan (an African child) meets the escaped monkey in a London street. "The black and the brown hugged each other as though they were long-lost brothers."

Later in the story, in Chapter 15, Part II, the African child and the monkey are in Regents Park. This leads to a supposedly hilarious scene in which the onlookers are unable to tell the difference between the black child and the monkey.

The subject changed to this latest book, *Friend Monkey.* Ms. Travers was annoyed that I had not yet read *Friend Monkey,* and she began to read to me from the book:

"Miss Brown-Potter was a female explorer, who now lived in retirement. Once, on a trip to Africa, she had rescued a baby from a crocodile on the banks of the River Tooma. He belonged, she had learned, to the Fan tribe, and since his family seemed not to want him — perhaps because the child was deaf — she had brought him back to England with her and named him after two famous explorers."

33

I asked Ms. Travers if she didn't think that having a black family reject a child and feed him to crocodiles because he is deaf would be offensive to black parents, especially in a children's book? She avoided my question by stating that this was an actual practice of the Fan tribe in Africa. [To the Council's best knowledge, the only Tooma River is in New South Wales — it should be noted here that Ms. Travers, who is considered an English author, was born and reared in Australia. Records consulted by the Council indicate that Fan is a variant spelling for the Fang of Gabon, in West Africa. However, the Council could find no substantiation for the assertion that the Fang leave handicapped children on river banks.]

"And why is the black boy speechless?" I asked.

"... because I do not presume to know what a black child of the Fan tribe in 1899 would be likely to say or think, and so by an imaginary device, he is speechless."

"Why must the child be black?" I asked. She replied that you do not find a white child on the River Tooma in Africa, whereupon I interjected that Tarzan was a white child found in Africa.

"That is the difference between imagination and fantasy," she answered.

It was apparent that the interview had come to an end. I put on my wellingtons and raincoat, said good-bye to P.L. Travers, and left. It was still raining, hard as ever.

Oh! Please Mr. Tiger

Janet Hill

In March, 1972, Chatto and Windus, publishers of *Little Black Sambo* and other books by Helen Bannerman, drew renewed attention to them by advertising a boxed set containing all seven volumes, which their catalogue claimed "deserves a place on every child's bookshelf". Subsequently, Brian Alderson wrote an article "Banning Bannerman" in his column in *The Times* following a statement on the books he had elicited from the Central Committee of Teachers against Racism (TAR), which had roundly condemned them as books "which foster racist attitudes in children". They also said "In all of these books the underlying racist message is made all the more sinister by their appearance of innocence and charm", and claimed that "Along with the whimsical stories the reader swallows wholesale a totally patronising attitude towards black people who are shown as greedy (Black Sambo eats 169 pancakes)...". The correspondence this article engendered in the columns of *The Times* was a predictable mixture of reasonable, hysterical and indignant letters.

I sympathise full with the aims of TAR, but I regret the no doubt hasty statement they made on *Little Black Sambo,* which left them wide open to ridicule because of the terms in which they criticised this book, which has been surrounded by controversy, particularly in the United States, for many years. Seen in isolation, their comment that black people are shown as greedy because Sambo at the end of his adventures eats 169 pancakes is clearly laughable to anyone who knows the story, and deserves to be treated with ridicule. Equally the sentence about the "underlying racist message" and the implication that this is not only "sinister" but deliberate shows a lamentable failure to acknowledge the historical context of the book. That TAR failed to take this factor into account is further shown by a comment in their letter to Brian Alderson, not quoted in his article, in which they claim that *"Little White Squibba* was clearly written as a conciliatory sop"*. This is to credit the author with low cunning as well as an awareness which would have made her thinking impossibly ahead of her time.

Helen Bannerman was born in Edinburgh, the daughter of an Army chaplain. When she was two, her family went to Madeira, where she stayed until the age of ten, when she was sent back to Scotland to be educated. In 1889 she married an Army doctor, and spent the next thirty years of her life in India. She wrote and illustrated *The Story of Little Black Sambo* for her two daughters in 1899, and it was published the same year. Another four titles had been published by 1909. *Sambo and the Twins* appeared in 1937, and *Little White Squibba* was published posthumously in 1966.

No one, least of all a librarian, could deny that her books are popular with children, and this is perfectly understandable. The stories have an engaging mixture of simplicity and absurdity which cannot fail to appeal, and show how well the author must have understood young children. There seems to be fairly general agreement that *Little Black Sambo* is by far the best of them, and it is the title mentioned in every reputable bibliography of children's books for the very young. Marcus Crouch in *Treasure Seekers and Borrowers* sums up succinctly:

> Throughout the history of children's literature, books have appeared which have had a success out of all proportion to their artistic merits. *Little Black Sambo,* crudely drawn, unpretentiously written, struck a chord to which children's hearts responded.

However, re-evaluation of books is a continual process. How do these books look in our multi-racial society now? I believe this a valid question to ask, despite Brian Alderson's comment in his article that "once external considerations are allowed to affect our criteria for judging texts, critical anarchy supervenes. Billy Bunter is banned because there are fat boys in Ipswich...''. To compare the attack on *Little Black Sambo* with an attack on Billy Bunter is hardly justified. There is no blatant prejudice against fat boys. They were not colonised, taken into slavery or treated as inferior. White letter writers to *The Times* wittily poured ridicule on the suggestion that *Little Black Sambo* is racist, on the grounds that they had never found it so, and some of them excelled at explaining how delightfully tolerant they were. Other writers expressed a different point of view:

> As a black Briton, born and educated in this country, I detested *Little Black Sambo* as much as I did the other textbooks which presented non-white people as living entirely in primitive conditions and having no culture.

I asked black people in Lambeth for their views. A women's group from a community association was extremely indignant, and found the books insulting to black people; they felt that the names chosen were typical of those used by white people to degrade black people; and that the stories were totally outdated. The strength of their feelings matched those of the writers to *The Times* who claimed that to dispense with these books would be censorship. A teacher at a large comprehensive school sent me a tape of a lively and good humoured discussion recorded by a group of black teenagers. They felt that everything about the books conveyed an image of the black man living in mud huts, and that the way the characters communicated with animals seemed to imply that they were inferior, and close to the animal world.

Asked about the names, they said it wasn't just the names, it was everything combined — the teeth and eyes, the "Al Jolson" feeling, always smiling, "Yes Sir, No Sir" — the whole idea of a smiling black, and the feeling that all you need to do to make him happy is to put a bunch of mangoes in front of him... They made very perceptive comments about the contrast between *Little Black Sambo* and *Little White Squibba,* by far the weakest of all the stories. They felt that in

the latter book everything was so *nice,* and that it was
noticeable that the animals were treated as pets. They also
contrasted the first meeting of Squibba and Sambo with their
respective tigers. When told by the tiger "I am going to eat
you up," Squibba says "All right, try my sash". Sambo,
faced by exactly the same situation, says "Oh! Please Mr
Tiger, don't eat me up and I'll give you my beautiful little
Red Coat" (always the picture of the docile nigger, they
commented). Unlike most critics, they clearly saw the books
in their historical context, and realised it was inevitable that a
woman of Helen Bannerman's background and period would
think and write as she did.

Marcus Crouch has called the illustrations "crudely
drawn". They certainly are. *Little Black Sambo* as shown in
full regalia on page 18 is a grinning stereotype with clownish
eyes and huge mouth; the old woman on page 11 of *Little
Black Quasha* turns round with a horrified face and her face
is horrifying; Black Mumbo and Black Jumbo on page 82 of
Sambo and the Twins jump for joy on hearing that the twins
are safe, looking for all the world like a caricature of two
cotton pickin' niggers in their gaily striped clothes. Admittedly
the illustrations in *Little White Squibba* are excruciatingly
badly drawn, but they are nice and dainty. To compare
Squibba in her full fingery of page 18 with the previously
mentioned picture of Sambo is to point up the difference. She
is unmistakably flesh and blood; a real human being with a
dignity and poise befitting her station in life. He is an unreal
caricature, less than human, with matchstick legs and golliwog
face. Certainly, as the text claims, they both look grand.
What is equally certain is that they inhabit different worlds.

Just as the illustrations are best discussed by contrasting
Little White Squibba and the other books, so is the text. Not
surprisingly the condescension of the writer is shown up most
clearly by Squibba. She is sent books for her birthday "about
little black children who had wonderful adventures in the
jungle", and wants to follow their example. Imitation may be
the sincerest form of flattery, but as the astute teenagers who
discussed the books pointed out, her experiences, although

superficially the same as Sambo's, are in fact quite different. She confronts each animal with aplomb, forestalls every move, and calmly invites them all, including the tiger, home to afternoon tea. They have pancakes, "because that was what most of the little black children had had after their adventures". Squibba is certainly secure in her tasteful and well-ordered home, where even the pancakes have a delicacy denied those served in the jungle. Meanwhile Sambo and his friends live on in their strange quasi-African jungle home, dancing around barefoot, surrounded by Indian tigers and eating mangoes and pancakes.

Seen in this light I believe that the stories are condescending and patronising. I would not cite individual incidents so much as the entire ambience of the books, particularly as thrown into relief by *Little White Squibba.* The ambience of a book is sometimes a difficult thing to pinpoint, as anyone who has tried to prove that the ambience of so many English children's books is comfortably middle-class will realise. I freely admit that my own views about these books have changed, and that I championed *Little Black Sambo* in print some years ago, so that I can recognise that it is probably difficult for those of us who are white and care about children's books to see them as other than charming little stories. To call Helen Bannerman consciously racist is absurd. However, to recognise that her books are just another expression of benevolent paternalism, the more insulting for its benevolence, is merely to show awareness of the deep roots of racism in our history, culture and language. Her *outlook* is certainly racist in the context of today.

Several letters to *The Times* pointed out gleefully that young black children enjoy these stories, and quoted this is a vindication of their racism. Sheila Ray makes the same point in her book *Children's Fiction.* I find this patently absurd. Four- and five-year-olds, whether black or white, are not generally noted for their perspicacity in identifying racism in books. However, black children gradually come to recognise how the white world sees them. A story told by Bernard Coard in a recent book *(How the West Indian Child is made*

Educationally Sub-Normal in the British School System)
should haunt us all. Appalled that a black child in his class
always drew and painted himself white, the author offered to
draw the child himself. When he drew him as he was, the boy
was deeply upset and said that he had been made to look like
a golliwog.

Helen Bannerman's books have had a long life, and the
time has come to consign them to oblivion. They should have
no place in a multi-racial society. What was it Marcus Crouch
said? "Throughout the history of children's literature, books
have appeared which have had a success out of all proportion
to their artistic merits." They have had a fuss out of all
proportion, too.

Charlie and the Chocolate Factory: A New Look at an Old Favourite

Lois Kalb Bouchard

It is significant to note that in response to criticism, the author and publisher have felt it necessary to make certain revisions in this book. In the 1973 edition, issued since the review which appears below, the Oompa-Loompas are no longer black and no longer from Africa. The revisions do mitigate the book's racism somewhat but they do not substantially change the negative values and oppressive attitudes conveyed by the book.

It has been several years since the publication of *Charlie and the Chocolate Factory* by Roald Dahl (Allen & Unwin 1967). Since it is still a widely selling children's book, a discussion of its racism is not inappropriate now. Although the black characters are treated in an approving manner, whereas several of the white characters are treated harshly, racism persists in the time-dishonoured stereotypes, in the childishness and the dependency upon whites of the black characters.

In this fantasy story, the owner of the chocolate factory, Mr. Willy Wonka, has to find factory workers who will not steal his candy-making secrets. He finds a tribe of "miniature pygmies" about the height of a man's knee in "the very deepest and darkest part of the African jungle where no white man had ever been before". The West has been treated to "dark Africa" too many times, and it is racism to perpetuate

41

the myth and its negative image of darkness. The people Wonka finds are called "Oompa-Loompas", an offensive name since it tries to make fun of African language sounds. And they are incompetent in jungle living — they are "practically starving to death". Wonka (the Great White Father) saves the Oompa-Loompas by taking them back home and giving them work.

Wonka offers the Oompa-Loompas cacao beans for their meals and wages. The fact that the Oompa-Loompas are delighted and willing to accept the beans shows their childishness and gullibility. But Wonka says about himself, "You don't think *I* live on cacao beans, do you?" Besides loving candy, the Oompa-Loompas are always laughing. They are presented as spirited, but as lacking dignity, getting "drunk as lords" on butterscotch and soda and "whooping it up".

The Oompa-Loompas are musical, with enough intelligence to write songs, which, moreover, contain the morals and messages of the book. However, the moralism embodied in the songs is fierce, and the Oompa-Loompas seem like Furies:

Veruca Salt, the little brute,
Has just gone down the garbage chute...
We've polished off her parents, too.

These make the Oompa-Loompas seem rather like self-righteous children — Furies, little bogeymen. They are still, then, within the purview of the stereotype — they make music, and moral music at that, but with the touch of the savage. Besides, after the songs, the black characters recede again into childishness, dependency and dehumanisation.

The element of savagery is further suggested by these lines from one of the songs:

... And cannibals crouching round the pot,
Stirring away at something hot.
(It smells so good, what can it be?
Good gracious, it's Penelope.)

42

The name "Penelope" suggests a white girl; the term "cannibals" suggests blacks. Still another racist note is the fact that the rich girl and her father refer to an Oompa-Loompa character as "it". The author may have intended to disparage the father and daughter by having them use the neuter pronoun; however, leaving such a thing questionably in the air is, at best, insensitivity.

As workers in the factory, the black characters are exploited. The owner clicks his fingers sharply when he wants a worker to appear. The Oompa-Loompas are made to test various kinds of candies, sometimes with unfortunate effects. For example, one man sprouts a beard that never stops growing. The only comment on this is, "In the end we had to use a lawn mower to keep it in check! But I'll get the mixture right soon!" The following example is worse still:

> "I gave some to an old Oompa-Loompa once out in the back yard and he went up and up and up and disappeared out of sight! It was very sad. I never saw him again."
>
> "He should have burped," Charlie said.
>
> "Of course he should have burped," said Mr. Wonka. "I stood there shouting, 'Burp, you silly ass, burp, or you'll never come down again!' But he didn't or couldn't or wouldn't, I don't know which. Maybe he was too polite. He must be on the moon by now."

It cannot be said that the Oompa-Loompas are treated any worse — in a satiric or caricature sense — than the white characters. The white children suffer fates far worse than their vices would seem to warrant (the girl who chews gum turns purple and remains purple; the TV watcher is ten feet tall at the end). However, the children's parents are concerned about their fates, and the children suffer individualised fates. But a black man floats away to his death stupidly silent, and no one among his family or friends misses him. As far as the book is concerned, the Oompa-Loompas are still laughing.

The paternalism toward the black workers is given a resounding finale. Says Mr. Wonka: *"Someone's* got to keep it (the factory) going — if only for the sake of the Oompa-Loompas..." It is this ending to the book that makes clear the racism present throughout. The entire plot is based on Wonka's quest for an heir — he has invited five children to his factory so that he can choose one. No black child is a contender, although there are 3,000 black people, many of them children, inside his factory. He searches the outside world for a child to become the owner. And although in the story he searches the "whole world", only preponderantly white-populated countries — Russia and England — are mentioned by name. The children who find the golden admission tickets are never designated white in words, but the illustrations show white children, and the Oompa-Loompas are designated black. Thus, the implication is that black characters are forever dependent upon the white boss. This message comes across in a particularly strong manner, because it is not verbalised and yet the whole plot rests upon it. It may be argued that the Oompa-Loompas are ruled out as heirs because of their size, not because of their colour, but this is not what comes across in the context of the story. Furthermore, it is quite possible that, in fact, the small size of the black characters becomes a symbol of their implied inadequacies.

The Cay: Racism Rewarded

Albert V. Schwartz

Rather than earn praise for literary achievement on behalf of "brotherhood", *The Cay* by Theodore Taylor (Bodley Head 1970, Puffin 1973) should be castigated as an adventure story for white colonialists — however enlightened — to add to their racist mythology. Four well-known review publications and five major book awards (including one "brotherhood" award) have brought *The Cay* extraordinary literary prominence.

The Cay is really the story of the initiation of a white upper middle class boy (Phillip, an American) into his "proper" role in a colonialist, sexist, racist society. The book itself is colonialist, sexist, and racist. It is colonialist because the author accepts that the people of Curaçao and most of the other Caribbean islands (the setting of the story) should be controlled and ruled by foreign powers.

The Cay also maintains the sexist tradition. The only woman in the story is a querulous, weak, subservient and fearful mother. It is, in fact, her fear of planes that results in the male hero of the story taking a ship, and the sinking of the ship sets in motion their adventures.

Racist values undergo minor change but meet no challenge in this book. Throughout the story, the white boy remains master, the black man subservient. Whenever, temporarily, the black man takes command, he does it "like a black mule", and only for the sake of the white boy's well-being.

The Cay is about eleven-year-old Phillip Enright, who is marooned on a small island (a cay) with an elderly West Indian, Timothy (no last name). Phillip, who relates the tale, has been living in the Caribbean because his father is an oil refining expert on loan to Royal Dutch Shell from a U.S.

company.

The first half of the book establishes Phillip as a bigoted young "Southern Cracker", but the reader knows from the outset that the author will slap Phillip down. Early in the book Phillip declares that his mother was brought up in Virginia and that "she didn't like them". "Them" are black people. Of the black Timothy, Phillip says, "he smelled different and strong," and he recoils from Timothy's touch. The black man's appearance, says Phillip, is "very much like the men I'd seen in the jungle pictures. Flat nose and heavy lips."

Midway through the book Phillip undergoes a conversion — or so the author would have us believe. This is the "character growth" of young Phillip that is supposed to contribute to the literature of "brotherhood". Were Phillip's racist attitudes to undergo substantive change, were he to really have his consciousness raised and grow in human understanding as a result of his close association with Timothy — all well and good. But this just doesn't happen. Phillip's growth is merely a shift in the direction of his racism.

Phillip's "conversion" stems from his loss of sight after he is shipwrecked, when he comes to depend on Timothy for help and protection. But the boy's dependency on the man (to be expected had they been of the same class and/or race) is here due only to an extraordinary occurrence, the boy's loss of sight. The conversion comes when Phillip — remember, now, he is blind — lies down next to Timothy and says, "he felt neither white nor black". Soon he is saying that Timothy is "kind". Then comes the question: "Timothy, are you still black?"

The author does not have Timothy answer loud and clear, "No, I am not white, I am black;" instead, Timothy obligingly laughs himself into anonymity.

True to the "liberal philosophy" of a bygone age, the *New York Times* review of *The Cay* made this glib comment on Phillip's question: "Phillip... realised that racial consciousness is merely a product of sight." As Timothy is made to say in

The Cay, "I true tink beneath d'skin is all d'same."

But all that Phillip's question really means is that he has begun to realise that blackness doesn't have to elicit the hatred and contempt his mother had taught him. He is beginning to find in one black man something acceptable to his own traditions and values, something that can elicit warmth and affection. But Phillip never gets past that. For him, the gap between them remains. He always judges Timothy by his own "superior" white values. Neither he nor the book ever come close to a real understanding of what Timothy's blackness is about; neither come close to facing, accepting, and therefore respecting blackness on its own terms. (The two ways of looking at the black experience have been pointed out by Ray Anthony Shepard, the author of *Sneakers* and other children's books. He contrasted the stories of the white author/illustrator Ezra Jack Keats, with their liberal insistence on human similarities and sameness, with those of the black author/illustrator John Steptoe, which celebrate the ethnic differences of blacks.)

Timothy, however, exists for the reader only as he is — and because he is — experienced by Phillip. The former's sole care has been the boy's survival, and he has proven himself equal — or almost so — to the task. He is good, kind, generous, resourceful and happy. True to stereotype, he is also somewhat dishonest, superstitious, and quite ignorant (he cannot read or write). Furthermore, Phillip at eleven knows a great deal of history, but the considerably older Timothy knows none. When asked about Africa, Timothy answers: "I 'ave no recollection o' anythin' 'cept dese islan's. 'Tis pure outrageous, but I do not remember anythin' 'bout a place called Afre-ca."

Outrageous? Yes. What should outrage us is that the book's author, its editor, and its publisher should foist upon our children such an image of a black man today!

Besides all this, Timothy is a black man who knows and keeps his place. Well-schooled in oppression and colonialism, he is very much aware that the system dictates that he call a white boy "young bahss". Only when the black has proven

47

himself by his care and attentiveness, and the white boy is no longer afraid of him, is Timothy given permission (which is granted, not assumed) to call the white boy by *his* first name.

In *The Cay,* Timothy is denied not only his colour. He is denied history, parents, family, children. He is denied all social ties except one, and that single tie is with a white boy, for whom in the end he is denied his life. Timothy dies before he and Phillip can be rescued from the cay, but conveniently only after he has taught Phillip the arts of survival and been the catalyst for Phillip's "conversion". After this, there is no need for him and therefore he has no future.

After his rescue, when Phillip goes back to Curaçao, he spends a lot of time at the Ruyterkade market "talking to the black people. I liked the sound of their voices. Some of them had known old Timothy from Charlotte Amalie. I felt close to them." Now "enlightened", Phillip condescends to mingle with some blacks at a market. His vision and commitment go no further.

One thing we are certain about. Phillip won't grow up to march with a Martin Luther King (to whose memory *The Cay* is dedicated). On the contrary, Phillip will return to his world, the world of his father and mother, a little wiser, but the world no better.

Sounder: A Black or a White Tale?

Albert V. Schwartz

In a recent exchange of letters with George Woods, the *New York Times* children's book editor, Julius Lester wrote: "When I review a book about blacks (no matter the race of the author), I ask two questions: 'Does it accurately present the black perspective?' 'Will it be relevant to black children?'"

Since the book *Sounder* by William H. Armstrong (Gollancz 1971) has achieved prominence as the 1970 recipient of the coveted John Newbery Medal award for the year's most distinguished book for children published in the United States, it merits literary analysis from many points of view. Lester's two questions represent an ideological approach, and it is from this approach that *Sounder* will be analysed.

Shelton L. Root, Jr., reviewing the book for *Elementary English* (May 1970), states: "As important literary social commentary, *Sounder* cannot be faulted." Root feels that the injustices narrated in the story will leave the reader "both indignant and guilty". This commentary is typical of the reviews that have appeared by white critics for white audiences. Surely this response by white people played a paramount role in the book's selection for the Newbery medal.

Mr. Armstrong states in his Author's Note that the actual story was told to him by a teacher, "a grey-haired black man". The note continues: "It is the black man's story, not mine... It was history — his history". Thus the author claims authentic black history originating in the perception and intelligence and "soul" of the black teacher, casting the white author in an entirely passive role. This claim, while undoubtedly made in good faith, does not bear up under examination.

Tom Feelings, in the Spring 1970 issue of *Interracial Books for Children,* questioned whether a black man could talk freely to a member of his oppressors at the time the story was first told. Mr Feelings stated that a story of the black experience must come directly from one who has lived it. Authenticity in this case hinges upon life experience.

The style of *Sounder* is white fundamentalist; the words, imagery, and philosophy are simple, direct and interwoven into the story are occasional religious tales offering hope of a "heavenly sanctuary". By contrast, the black spirituals — "Swing Low, Sweet Chariot" and "Steal Away to Jesus" — embody a struggle for freedom and a hope for a better life here on earth. The music of Sounder's family is more "white spiritual" than "blues". Black language, a vital and historic means of communication for the creation of a story of black people, is totally absent.

Whose fault is this? Did the black teacher talk the language he thought the white man would understand? Could it be that the white man who listened failed to hear the subtle tones that were spoken to him? Or is it possible that *Sounder* is a highly commercial package in synthetic garb?

Why is no one in the sharecropper's family identified by a name, except, the dog, Sounder? Did the black story-teller really narrate the story without names?

Within the white world, deep-seated prejudice has long denied human individualisation to the black person. At the time of the story's historical setting, white people avoided calling black people by their names; usually they substituted such terms as uncle, auntie, boy, Sambo; or they called every black person by the same name. The absence of name helped to avoid the use of the polite salutation.

This black family, as anonymous as the original teller of the tale, are Sounder's family, and can only be so identified. Within the family, only the "boy" (itself a term implying immaturity) exists independently. The others exist simply in relationship — "mother", "father", "children". The adults are successfully denied authority. This anonymity, then, represents the successful imposition of a white point of view upon the story.

It is, furthermore, difficult to believe that the picture presented even begins to grasp at the reality of the situation — and, as if to confirm this, the characters refuse to spring to life, and remain shadowy and unreal.

Black militancy today is forcing whites to consider blacks as human beings, but at the time the story took place, blacks were often assumed incapable of such human emotion as suffering. If they suffered at all in the literature of the Southern Tradition, they did so in silence.

In *Sounder,* only the dog expresses reaction and bitterness. The author actually calls the dog a "human animal". When the father is taken away by the sheriff, the dog angrily rushes in pursuit, and by that expressive act risks its life and is shot. The mother, the boy, and the other children say and do *nothing.* There is a minimal display of emotion even after the sheriff and his deputies have long gone. Compare the reaction of the children when their dog is taken away! The implication seems to be that black children care more about their animals than their parents.

One could suggest that the emphasis on concern for the dog is a symbol for the concern the family might have for the father. However, the feelings for the dog are so direct and straightforward that the "symbolic" theory is hard to accept. Also, any anguish the mother might feel is likewise only faintly implied.

W.E.B. Du Bois wrote *The Souls of Black Folk* in the same historical setting as *Sounder.* Here is how Du Bois presented the black sharecropper: "I see now that ragged black man sitting on a log, aimlessly whittling a stock. He muttered to me with the murmur of many ages, when he said: 'White man sit down whole year; Nigger work day and night and make crop; Nigger hardly gits bread and meat; white man sitting down gits it all. It's *wrong.*'"

Never once in *Sounder* do you meet the white owner of the land. The oppression results from the poverty of the land and the cruelty of the penal institution. Yet the father is crushed,

51

not by the mean prison guard, but by a chance "act of God".

True to the white Southern fundamentalism of the author, the "boy" meets up with no activist. His hope lies in getting an education. Suddenly, after his father is taken from him, the boy manages to go to school, where he studies the words of Montaigne. "Only the unwise think that what has changed is dead," says that author. White paternalism forbids that a black boy should learn from any but a white author-philosopher.

Sounder's family is isolated; there is no relationship with other black people, except an occasional preacher. The Bible stories which the black mother tells are exclusively white Baptist fundamentalism — and very racist. Her Bible stories have none of the qualities of black Biblical interpretation, and so we hear the mother telling her son: "Some people is born to keep. Some is born to lose. *We was born to lose,* I reckon." (Italics added).

The mother in the story *is* the black stereotype of the Southern Tradition. Toward her children she shows no true feeling, no true compassion — strictly a Southern interpretation of black motherhood. After her son makes great sacrifices to go to school, she even discourages him from going. Another time, after he has searched for his dog for hours, she admonishes him coldly: "You're hungry, child. *Feed yourself."* This mother is divested of "soul", a quality a black writer today would assuredly have recognised and given her.

Lerone Bennett, Jr., in his criticism of William Styron's *The Confessions of Nat Turner,* said of white writers emasculating black families: "First of all, and most important of all, there is a pattern of emasculation, which mirrors America's ancient and manic pattern of de-balling black men. There is a second pattern, which again mirrors the white man's praxis, a pattern of destructuring the black family..." Bennett's statement applies equally to *Sounder.*

In the light of this analysis of *Sounder,* the response must be no to Lester's two questions: "Does it accurately present the black perspective?" and "Will it be relevant to black children?'' A wholehearted affirmation must be given to Lester's next contention: ''The possibility of a book by a white answering these questions affirmatively is nil.''

The Slave Dancer: Critiques of a Newbery Award Winner

The Slave Dancer *by Paula Fox (Macmillan 1974, Piccolo 1977) won the American Library Association's Newbery Award in 1974 as the preceding year's "most distinguished" children's book, although it is filled with a subtle yet pervasive racism. On the following pages, four authors address the racism in the book: two — Binnie Tate and Sharon Bell Mathis — are black, two — Lyla Hoffman and Albert V. Schwartz — are white. The comments by Ms. Mathis are taken from the presentation at the Council for Interracial Books for Children's seminar on racism and sexism in children's books at that year's ALA convention.*

Racism and Distortions Pervade "The Slave Dancer"
Binnie Tate

Having a good deal of respect for some of the author's earlier writings, I approached *The Slave Dancer* by Paula Fox with positive expectations. After reading the book, I pushed my nagging negative feelings into the background. Later, during conversations and discussions about the book, my apprehensions kept surfacing. Much that was said about the book in these discussions had very racist implications, and these implications were supported by the book. I then reread *The Slave Dancer* to determine the reason for this.

At the American Library Association presentation by the Council in July, Sharon Bell Mathis vividly pointed out many of the negative aspects of the story. I support her findings and would like to suggest that no matter what the author's intent, this book presents grave problems for those of us concerned with eliminating children's materials which help perpetuate racism.

Told in the first person, *The Slave Dancer* is the story of Jessie Bollier, a thirteen-year-old boy who is shanghaied and compelled to work on a slave ship. The title derives from the boy's shipboard assignment to play his fife and "dance" the slaves, which was in essence an exercise to keep the slaves alive.

Most of the story takes place aboard ship. The crew is described, and several scenes revolve around their interaction with the boy and each other. Later, the slaves are brought aboard and Jessie and the crew are seen in relation to the slaves.

The tainted ship meets with disaster. Jessie and Ras, a slave boy, are the only survivors. They swim to shore where they meet an escaped slave who takes care of them. Ras is taken to safety and Jessie returns home.

In the early passages of the story, the captain of the ship speaks of Jessie as "creole". This identification could be thoroughly confusing to readers. Depending upon a person's background, "creole" may have a variety of meanings. For some, it means anyone in the colonies with a European background; for others, it is a French-Spanish, French-English or French-American mixture. In the Black community, "creole" generally implies some basis in blackness — for example, a black person from a certain area of Louisiana with creole parentage and who speaks creole or any white-skinned black.

In any case, some readers identify the main character as creole black and others identify him as creole white. Certainly, the interpretation of the story will differ accordingly.

As the story develops the author attempts to portray the slave ship's captain and crew as villains, but through the characters' words, she excuses the captors and places the blame for the slaves' captivity on Africans themselves. The author slowly and systematically excuses almost all the whites in the story for their participation in the slave venture and by innuendo places the blame elsewhere. A few examples follow:

> The native chiefs are so greedy for our trade goods, they sell their people cheaper than they ever did to tempt us to run the British blockade. (page 34)

> I thought of the African kings setting upon each other's tribes to capture the men and women — and children for all I knew — who would be bartered for spirits and tobacco and arms... (page 59)

> The chiefs kidnap the children... The slavers give good trade goods for them because they fetch such high prices in the West Indies. (page 71)

The following quotes were probably an attempt to balance this perspective, but they are too feeble and have an almost equally negative impact:

> Purvis had said the native kings sold their own people willingly, yet he'd also told me there were chiefs who would sink the ship and kill us if they had the chance. (page 53)

> The African was tempted and then became depraved by a desire for the material things offered him by debased traders. (page 71)

America is held generally blameless in the slave trade. Says Jessie, "I learned then that there were American laws, too, against the importing of slaves" (page 39). Later in the book, the Americans are compared favourably with the Spanish. When the slaves are forced to dress up, a crew member says, "[The slaves] ought to have a bit of pleasure before the Cubans get them. The Spanish are very cruel you know" (page 111). The British are also at least partly exonerated: "They've entirely stopped the slave trade in their country" (page 34).

On page 60 the author attempts to equate the African slave trade with other historical incidents. Says one of the crew:

Do you think it was easier for my own people who sailed to Boston sixty years ago from Ireland, locked up in a hold for the whole voyage where they might have died of sickness and suffocation?... and you dare speak of my parents in the same breath with these niggers!

The plight of the crew is described as worse than that of the slaves:

[The captain was] terrible, terrible with his crews, and only a little less so with the blacks. But he wants *them* in good health to make his profit. But God help the sick nigger for he'll drop him overboard between the brandy and the lighting of his pipe! (pages 31-32)

In scenes aboard ship, the crew are generally portrayed as vile, coarse and vicious but the author even manages to cancel these qualities in most of the crew.

But except for Stout and Spark and the Captain, the men were *not especially cruel* save in their shared and unshakeable conviction that the least of them was better than any black alive. Gardere and Purvis and Cooley even played with the small black children... (italics added, page 81)

The slaves in the story are completely dehumanised. They are often spoken of as "creatures". Many of the statements and incidents regarding them are prejudicial and totally unnecessary to the development of the story. Some of the statements and incidents which are seemingly included only to "colour" the blacks follow:

I won't have Ibos. They're *soft as melons* and kill themselves if they're not watched twenty-four hours a day.

57

I will not put up with such *creatures!* (italics added, page 28)

The slaves are *never* gone!... All of Africa is nothing but a bottomless sack of blacks. (page 54)

... the *poor poor* black fellows. Poor indeed! Living in savagery and ignorance. Think on this — their own chiefs can't wait to throw them in our holds! (page 55)

They [the slaves] ain't like us, and that's the truth. (page 65)

... since none of [the slaves] were Christian he would not *corrupt his tongue* by learning a single word from any of them. (italics added, page 71)

Most striking are comments from the boy Jessie:

I hated the slaves! I hated their shuffling, their howling, their very suffering. I hated the way they spat out their food upon the deck, the overflowing buckets, the emptying of which tried all my strength. I hated the foul stench that came from the holds no matter which way the wind blew, as though the ship itself were soaked with human excrement. I would have snatched the rope from Spark's hand and beaten them myself! Oh God! I wished them all dead! Not to hear them! Not to smell them, not to know of their existence. (page 78)

Aside from the constantly repeated racist implications and negative allusions, there is a question of *The Slave Dancer's* historical accuracy. There is, for instance, some question about the slaves being "Ashantis captured in tribal wars with the Yoruba". I can find no evidence of these being warring peoples.

Certainly there is not enough evidence that African chiefs were a *primary* force in the slave trade to allow for the consistent projection of this theme.

One may also argue the credibility of the relationship that is portrayed between Jessie and the slave boy Ras. There was no basis for the trust which exists between them in the final passages of the story.

The author has assumed the task of dealing in this story with a serious and critical issue in U.S. history. Slavery touches at the very "gut" of the black experience in America, and young children deserve a *fair* and *accurate* picture of it, even in a work of fiction. Instead, as presented, this story has clearly racist leanings.

The Newbery-Caldecott Committee of the ALA has given this book a label of excellence. It therefore becomes the responsibility of adults who care about the eradication of racism to reject the purchase and use of *The Slave Dancer.*

Evaluating Books by New Criteria

Lyla Hoffman

I'm white. The Council invited me to read *The Slave Dancer* and join a discussion of the book. So I read — I cried — and I went to the meeting.

I said to the Council discussion group (Asian, black and white women and men): "Paula Fox writes well. She wanted to do an expose of the 'middle passage' aspect of slavery. Young readers will learn from her book about the horrors of the slave trade. They will see the vileness of the whites who earned their livelihood from this 'human cargo'. I would be delighted to have children read this book."

The ensuing discussion did something more important than change my outlook on this particular well-intentioned book. The discussion forced me to formulate my own criteria for judging the worth of any children's book. In reaching my personal formulation, I had to abandon as irrelevant any

59

consideration of the *intent* of the author (or the *intent* of the librarians who gave it the Newbery award). I had to focus on the impact of the book on readers of *all* colours in today's racist society.

So when a black librarian, who is also a parent and a grandparent, spoke at that Council discussion, she set me thinking when she said, "Any black child reading *The Slave Dancer* would cringe at the endless, ugly remarks white characters spew out about the captured Africans. Black children must no longer be forced to hear such insults."

I suddenly realised that setting age-old racist remarks into fresh print today cannot be justified, especially when nothing else in the book counteracts the insulting "niggerisms". Even when the characters responsible for the insults are clearly described as evil and unsympathetic, their remarks still have the ability to wound young black readers deeply. And if an author intends to show that human oppression dehumanises the white oppressors as well as the oppressed blacks, then it is necessary to delineate the humanity of the blacks. This never was done in *The Slave Dancer*.

In thinking about the book's impact on black youngsters, I began to realise how white youngsters of today have also been socialised in a racist society. They too have been taught to believe vile things about blacks. They have been taught to feel virtuous when they feel compassion for the suffering of the oppressed. And they are taught to feel compassion without feeling the need to *do* anything about oppression. Jessie, the young hero of *The Slave Dancer,* feels horror and pity, but he does nothing as a boy; and he does nothing, later in life, as a man. He is, therefore, just part of the problem.

My new test of a book is: "Will this book advance human liberation or will it reinforce oppression?" Or, as a wise man previously put it, "If you're not part of the solution, you're part of the problem." Though I had long applied this yardstick to matters of personal behaviour, of school policy, of legal matters, of life in general — I had not had the sense to apply it to book criticism.

Although I have heard many compelling reasons for

condemning the choice of *The Slave Dancer* as a prize winner in the year 1974, the arguments were not necessary for me. I had switched. Today, my first test for evaluating a book is, "Will this book be part of the solution?"

An Insult to Black Children
Sharon Bell Mathis

I had hoped that Rosa Guy's *The Friends* would win the Newbery prize this year since it had been nominated. I thought, "Well, maybe this will be the year in the 53-year-history of the prize that a black book will win." *The Friends* did not win.

So this year *again* the ALA has chosen as "a distinguished book" one that insults my children and, yes, all black people. A book that perpetuates stereotypes about Africa and about blacks in general — stereotypes that in my writing I do my best to demolish.

Of course, I am talking as one black writer, but I am sure this is what all black writers who are writing for children today are about. Those of us who are writing for children are trying to celebrate and to document black truth.

Just in case there are some of you who haven't yet read *The Slave Dancer,* there are some excerpts that I would like to read to you from this year's "most distinguished book" for children.

> I wonder where [the slaves] think they are [says Jessie]. They don't think much answers [one of the crew]. (page 103)

> I saw the others regarded the slaves as less than animals, although having a greater value in gold... [and the crew shared an] unshakeable conviction that the least of them was better than any black alive. (page 81)

And if a white child never thought that before, it's in his head now.

They're all mad, the blacks! (page 55)

[The buckets are] latrines for the blacks... Put them where your fancy strikes you. It won't matter to *them*. (page 61)

Man?... you mean the nigger! (page 65)

Cawthorne [the captain] knew the black would recover — they can survive floggings that would kill a white man a hundred times over... (page 86)

And there's one thing I noticed in *The Slave Dancer*, nobody says anything about the white sailors taking a bath. One bucket of water per day is allotted to the *whole* crew for washing (page 36) but there's no attention given to that. Only to the fact that the smell that was on the ship came from black people.

And again, when the slaves are brought on board, "I heard a sound as though a thousand rats were scrambling up the hull of *The Moonlight*" (page 61). OK, now I know what it's like to sit at a typewriter half the night and look for the images that will say most what you want to say. And I just think that the word "rats" there was uncalled for. The feet of people don't sound like the feet of rats. Rats have a delicate sound. I know.

And then on page 111, you have, "Give what he calls a ball... [The captain] says the niggers like to dress up." And I want you to know, for those of you who haven't read the book" one that insults my children and, yes, all black people. "clothes... the very best! Silks, laces..." and I want you also to know that they had mentioned that the slaves of course couldn't wash. They were stinking terribly. They even had faeces sticking to their bodies. So if you have a trunk full of clothes that you have used again and again for these slaves that you dress up, and they all have human faeces on them, that's a tremendous expense, isn't it? To put these fine silks on people, and take them off, and clean them, or what have you, and put them back in the trunk. Well, I don't believe it. About this scene I thought, "How could somebody sit at a typewriter and write this, and then the ALA calls it 'distinguished'?" It isn't even believable.

And then you have a ship wreck, and the only two people to survive are the white boy and the black boy. And no sooner are they on land than the white child becomes the superior, the leader.

When a Newbery winner is cited, it is one of the first books that school officials make *sure* the children read. I have three children, one almost fifteen, one eleven and one nine, and they'll have to read "niggers like to dress up", they stink, they shuffle, they sound like rats coming on ships, and the reason why they're on the ship is because somebody black sold them out.

The ALA has a responsibility to *all* of us since libraries belong to all of us. And if libraries reflect what we are about, then there must be something wrong with us when librarians cite books like *Sounder* and *The Slave Dancer* as "distinguished".

Children's books have always reflected the society they flourished in. There was a time when people thought that books had to be very tiny because children were very small. We laugh about that now, but that was very serious at one time. "Little books for little people." There was another time when children had to read the most terrible, the most frightening literature, to make them good, to make them courteous, to make them understand that God was important. Now we all recognise the mistakes. I wonder, years from now, what people will recognise as *our* mistakes.

The Black Experience as Backdrop for White Adventure Story
Albert V. Schwartz

Should a white author use the black experience as mere background for a white-orientated adventure story?

This is one of several disturbing questions that have been posed by the selection of Paula Fox's *The Slave Dancer* for the 1974 Newbery Award.

For an analysis of *The Slave Dancer,* I would like to borrow some perspectives and criteria from Paul Hazard — the noted historian and author of *Books, Children and Men.*

To the question "What are good books for children?" Hazard answered,

> ... books that awaken in them not maudlin sentimentality, but sensibility; that enable them to share in great human emotions; that give them respect for universal life... that contain a profound morality. Not the kind of morality which consists in believing oneself a hero because one has given two cents to a poor man... here snivelling pity, there a pietism that knows nothing of charity; somewhere else a middle-class hypocrisy. Not the kind of morality that asks for no deeply felt consent, for no personal effort... books that set in action truths worthy of lasting forever, and of inspiring one's whole inner life...

With Hazard's concepts in mind — "Not maudlin sentimentality, but sensibility... inspiring one's whole inner life" — let us discuss *The Slave Dancer.*

The book revolves essentially around the familiar theme of a white adolescent boy's initiation into manhood. The location of young Jessie's ritual is the slave ship *The*

Moonlight. The evil white officers and crew are the masters of the ritual. The baptism occurs when Jessie emerges from the shipwrecked vessel as "the man", mastering the crisis and automatically assuming the leadership role in his relation with the one surviving black.

As Ruth Hill Viguers pointed out in *A Critical History of Children's Literature* (Macmillan, 1953):

> Over and over again, in sea adventure stories, is to be found the plot involving the young apprentice who must make his way among seasoned, often cruel seamen...

What is new in this particular sea adventure is the introduction of the black experience. The trade in African slaves becomes the backdrop for a white child's ritual. There are sea adventure stories in which galley "slaves" (English, Spanish, French) actively take over the ship and become the heroes, sometimes knighted by a European king. There are no such heroes in *The Slave Dancer.* In this sea story, chained black people passively submit to the whims of white men. By the story's end, all the blacks are destroyed, with the exception of one lone young boy. And he submits to the young white hero.

Millions of black people were killed during the "middle of a writer's attention, but Paula Fox describes only a hopeless acceptance of chains, beatings and humiliations.

For a white author to overcome the limitations of ethnocentric bias in an attempt to describe and interpret the black experience would be a challenging task. It would require a new creative approach to the polarisations of black and white views of historical reality. Such a white author would have to dig into the prevalent myths and stereotypes on a personal level — confront her or his own racism as a white person socialised in a racist society. An awesome task; but one that authors intent on portraying with truth an experience outside their own must strive for. (Here I want to say that previously, in *Blowfish Live in the Sea,* Paula Fox used reality with brilliance. In that story the one "real" fact illuminates

and defines the characters and the plot, and a moment of life
is revealed.)

In *The Slave Dancer,* the black victims are a nameless
mass, differentiated only by their sex. In other sea stories
white galley "slaves" would have names and personalities.
Here, no human characteristic is delineated for the slaves; no
individuality is shown. The whites in the story — despite their
evilness — possess names, possess personalities, possess
individualities. Their depravity is counteracted by their
"human" aspects. The Black people are *only* pathetic sufferers.
No "fight back" qualities whatever are found in these
characterless, chained objects on the ship *The Moonlight.* For
them the author presents no balance.

White writers frequently resort to the device of portraying
blacks as a passive, faceless mass to show their oppression.
The device is effective sometimes in creating pity and
sentimentality, but it is still dehumanising, and that is a major
flaw.

Paula Fox infers that whites and blacks participated equally
in the slave trade. This is another of the modern
manifestations of racism — to mitigate white responsibility
for slavery by blaming the victim. This white perspective
ignores the difference between chattel slavery in the U.S. —
which developed out of a desire for a massive supply of cheap
labour — and the slavery which existed in Africa. In Africa,
slaves were not considered biologically or culturally inferior;
they lived with the family they served; often their freedom
was assured after a certain number of years or they could buy
their way out of slavery; they could marry a non-slave and
not risk the loss of their children. Contemporary prejudices
are so often confused with historical truths!

One example of the put-down of blacks is the author's
unconscious bias in her use of proper nouns — capitalising a
noun and hence giving it dignity when the reference is to a
white person but lower-casing the noun and depriving it of
dignity when the reference is to a black. Read the following
paragraph from *The Slave Dancer* (page 59), and see if the
white captain and the African king, who are equated in

cruelty by the author, are given equal dignity in the writing:

> ... the [African] king and the Captain had got so drunk
> that when dawn rose, the Captain had clambered over the
> side, ready to make off and rule the tribe and leave the
> black king in command of the ship.

Jessie, the hero of this tale, never achieves Paul Hazard's concept of a "higher morality" which might "inspire inner life". Jessie's experience with oppression on the slaver simply inactivates him. He shows that he is aware of oppression but makes no meaningful protest; he takes no stand against it. He is no model for today's young readers. At the end of the ritual of baptism, Jessie cannot play his fife, thus easing the uncomfortable memories.

Despite endless incidents of white cruelty to blacks and of white cruelty to other whites, it is only when Jessie hears that African kings sell slaves that he is moved to think, "The world, I told myself, was as wicked a place as our parson had said..." (page 60). This line serves as the "moral" of the tale and it is the stepping stone for Jessie's defeatism as an adult. Jessie uses his privilege as a white to erase the ugly memories of his experience on the slaver. (In the anticlimactic ending of the book, Jessie states almost parenthetically that he was prepared for the horrors of the Civil War by his experience on *The Moonlight*.)

In the midst of his onerous jobs aboard ship — he is after all a kidnapped victim himself — he does not turn against the evil captain or the despicable crew but against the enslaved blacks: "I hated the slaves! I hated their shuffling, their howling, their very suffering" (page 78).

Later when Jessie is punished with five strokes of the whip he thinks:

> But one thing was clear, I was a thirteen-year-old male, not
> as tall though somewhat heavier than a boy close to my
> own age, now doubled up in the dark below, not a dozen
> yards from where I was being beaten. (page 79)

So Jessie's lot is not so bad — as long as others have it worse! White misery is not bad if black slavery is worse. It is an interesting psychological mechanism.

White readers who empathise with the misery of the black experience can feel virtuous. To feel virtuous is to feel superior. To put it into the terms of an R.D. Laing "Knot" or paradox: "I feel bad that this is happening to them. I feel good that I feel bad." But by thus feeling compassion, whites are relieved of the need to change society. Like Jessie, they end up feeling no real obligation to take a positive role. They merely take the passive role of not playing the fife — of not reacting to injustice in any meaningful way.

The Slave Dancer is an excellent example of the subtle forms literary racism has taken recently. (*Literary racism* may be defined as the aspect of cultural racism which deals with language, metaphors and mythology and which prevents a black-white unity capable of destroying institutional racism.)

If literature — just like every human institution and art form — can be a tool for oppression or a tool for liberation, then let us ask:

1. If a story emphasises the black experience, should it ever be written by anyone other than a black author?

2. Should the black experience ever be treated solely as a backdrop to a white historical panorama?

3. When a story includes the black experience, shouldn't authors and critics reject placing black survival and destiny in white hands? (For instance, should Ras, the young black boy, have immediately followed Jessie's leadership after the shipwreck?)

4. Should Third World people in any story written today be nameless and without individuality?

5. Should stories about the black experience produce in young people the kind of pity and guilt that results in

paternalistic attitudes? Shouldn't an inspired desire for human improvement, based upon truth and justice, be the product of good, anti-racist literature?

In conclusion I should like to offer another statement from Paul Hazard, who made the point so well:

> But to misshape young souls, to profit by a certain facility that one may possess to add to the number of indigestible and sham books... that is what I call oppressing children.

Children's Books and The Search for Black Identity

Rae Alexander

In 1970 I revised a recommended book list for the
N.A.A.C.P.* Based on the books I read in the course of
compiling that list, I draw this conclusion: Despite the
growing number of books depicting the black experience, the
image they give of the black American is still one of the more
insidious influences that hinder the black child from finding
true self-awareness.

In evaluating multiracial books for pre-school through
sixth-grade levels, my major criterion was that no book would
be listed if it was considered likely to communicate to either a
black or a white child a racist concept or cliché about blacks.
Even one negative stereotype would be enough to eliminate an
otherwise good book. It would also not be listed if it failed to
provide some strong characters to serve as role models.

One might say that the basic consideration in my not
including a given book in the N.A.A.C.P. list was the pain it
might give to even one black child. Naturally, there were
additional criteria. The book must be appropriate for use in
(1) an all-black classroom, (2) an all-white classroom, and (3)
an integrated classroom. If a book did not completely satisfy
each of these criteria, I excluded it from the bibliography.
Underlying these criteria was my own experience with many
teachers who are insensitive to the racist content of books or
who are not equipped to handle such material adequately in
their classes. The tragedy is that so many teachers fail to

* National Association for the Advancement of Coloured
People.

expose racist material for what it is, and they fail to make use
of it as a basis for discussing prejudice. To illustrate how
these standards were applied, I will discuss why I did not
include several books in the list.

A number of poignant and stirring stories I did not list
because they were marred by racial slurs. Even such an
imaginative and exciting story as L.M. Boston's *Chimneys of
Green Knowe* (Faber 1958, Puffin 1976) I excluded because of
a derogatory description of a black boy's hair: "Think of
Jacob's crinkly hair, hardly the length of a needle. The most
she could do with it [in her embroidery] was tediously to
make knots." In contrast the author refers to a white person's
"tresses": "... he was a vain man with hair he was proud
of... There was enough of Caxton's hair to do the whole
chimney."

is a delightful and charming story. However, on the first page
one reads, "only a small tuft of kinky hair showed from one
end..." In *A Sundae with Judy,* by Frieda Friedman
(Scholastic Book Services), the author writes, "She hadn't
noticed how dark Barbara and Bob Williams were, or how
much Mayling's eyes were slanted..." I did not list either of
these books, despite their many fine qualities.

I do not know whether passages such as those quoted above
express prejudice on the authors' part, but I do know that in
white America they reflect the language of racism, and that is
what children hear. I freely admit that in winnowing books, I
was primarily concerned with what the child would be
receiving. I was on the child's side, all the way. The black
child reading passages like those mentioned here surely senses
that his appearance is being unfavourably described, and that
is hardly conducive to strengthening self-esteem. One has only
to imagine how the child must feel when such slights are read
aloud in the presence of white classmates. Equally important,
how must they condition the white child's concept of blacks?

A problem of another kind arose in connection with books
that reflect the recent and entirely well-intentioned emphasis
on offering children material about American life as it really
is. One must consider the effect of this realism on the positive

self-image we want black children to develop. Blacks in the ghetto struggle with life from the day they are born. It is true that ghetto youngsters often find those books that are favoured in the suburbs pallid fare. However, the portrayal of ghetto life in "realistic" books is often overwhelmingly negative. There *are* hurtful parents, broken homes, and emotionally nonsupportive friends and teachers. These are facts of life, and the children who face them must cope as best they can. On the other hand, I believe that the constant depiction of ghetto society in this light is destructive — both of black children's view of themselves and of white children's understanding.

For essentially this reason, I excluded the much admired books of Frank Bonham. Two in particular — *The Nitty Gritty* and *The Mystery of the Fat Cat* (both E.P. Dutton) — emphasise a demoralising, decadent side of black life, which in these books is always, alas, overcome only by the direct or indirect intervention of *The Man*.

For much the same reason, I did not include the autobiography *It's Wings That Make Birds Fly,* edited by Sandra Weiner (Pantheon Books). Ten-year-old Otis tells his story in his own words, which Ms. Weiner recorded. It is a story of a broken home, punitive adults, overcrowded housing, inadequate play facilities, harassment of younger by older children, and the eternal benevolence of whites toward blacks. A paragraph at the end of the book states that Otis was killed in an accident while playing in the street.

I do not doubt the human truth of this autobiography, nor, in more general terms, do I question its social accuracy. But in the unrelievedly bleak and dismal portrayal of lower class black life, this book takes no notice of the fact that many blacks do possess personal values and that they do have the will and strength to help their children strive to master their environment — qualities that, as it happens, are usually unnoticed and unsupported by teachers and administrators. For the young white reader, this book supports prevailing stereotypes, and it offers no insight at all into the "hows" and "whys" of ghetto life. For the young black reader, the book too strongly affirms that all the Otises of today are doomed from birth.

Of the books that do foster a healthy self-image in the young black reader, I should like to mention three. *Bimby,* by Peter Burchard (Coward-McCann), is an historical novel set in the Sea Islands, off Georgia, just before the Civil War. Although young Bimby has not experienced slavery directly, through the mature wisdom of the old slave Jesse, he comes to understand what it means to be a man, and that he must himself find his own freedom. The author's illustrations enhance the story's underlying wistfulness and sadness. Black youth will find Bimby a strong image with which to identify.

Canalboat to Freedom, by Thomas Fall (Dial Press), vividly portrays the life of an ex-slave, Lundius, who risks death to help his black brothers escape to freedom via the underground railroad. He meets and befriends a white indentured servant named Benja, who is young and inexperienced in the ways of the world. Lundius helps Benja and others in practical, protective ways, but he is also a symbol of strength for them; it is his qualities as a man that so powerfully affect others and that enable Benja to carry on the work of Lundius after he is killed.

Bimby and *Canalboat to Freedom* stand apart from the general fare of children's books on slavery in several important respects. Bimby and Lundius are luminous, three-dimensional characters, very real and very much alive. Both possess an inner strength that enables them to strike out at the system in a positive way. Both are figures drawn from historical experience, and they will foster respect and pride in black children today.

Member of the Gang, by Barbara Rinkoff (Crown Publishers), is a story of today. The young black hero, Woodie Jackson, feels he amounts to little at home, in school, and at the settlement house where he spends his afternoons. His father is hardworking, gruff and stern; his mother is gentle but overprotective. Woodie jumps at the chance to join the Scorpions, because he thinks membership in the gang will make him important to himself and others. Following the inevitable street clash, arrest, and appearance in Family Court, Woodie is assigned a black probation officer who gives Woodie the kind of encouragement and support that parents and teachers have failed to provide. Together they build a new perspective on Woodie's life, and for Woodie the world takes on a very different meaning. The black-and-white illustrations by Harold James dramatically interpret Woodie's shifting moods and feelings. There are many Woodie Jacksons in our world, and the author has captured their reality in the central character. While Woodie's parents have negative qualities, the reader is allowed to see that their attitudes are expressions of their concern and love for their son. The black probation officer projects a strong black image.

In considering the constructive potential of books for children, one does not ask that they be antiseptic in portraying harsh realities; but one does ask that authors play a positive role by helping black children to better know their own strengths and power to bring about change. One hopes, too, that all authors — both black and white — will increasingly foster awareness and sensitivity in their young readers.

The Image of Gypsies In Children's Literature

Carla Stevens

In 1973, a 24-page document dealing with the plight of
European Gypsies was published by the Minority Rights
Group, a London-based organisation (36 Craven St., London
WC2N 5NG). The study criticises Western Europe for its
treatment of Gypsies and praises Yugoslavian attempts to
improve Gypsies' living standards.

There are over four million Gypsies in Europe, and their
birthrate is 2 to $3\frac{1}{2}$ per cent a year. These statistics, along with
the growing awareness of the plight of national minorities, are
forcing countries to re-examine their policies concerning the
nomadic people.

In France, for example, 90 per cent of Gypsy children are
illiterate. In Barcelona, Gypsy campsites have been destroyed
by the authorities in order not to offend American tourists. In
Switzerland over 700 children have been locked up in
institutions and kept from contact with their parents.

Only in Yugoslavia are there official attempts to encourage
Gypsies to participate in regional government activities. At the
same time, Gypsies from Eastern Europe are being pressured
to give up their nomadic life style and "adapt", to integrate
into the majority society.

Grattan Puxon, a founder of the British Gypsy Council and
spokesman for European Gypsies, has called for international
recognition that Gypsies are a separate people with a separate
way of life, united in a love for freedom which is based upon
their nomadic existence. Puxon's organisation has called for
the development of caravan schools, for the standardisation
of the Romany language to be taught in those schools, and
for the establishment of an international Romany language

newspaper. Above all, they call for support of the Gypsies' continued resistance to adopting the life style of non-nomadic people.

No one knows exactly how many Gypsies live in the U.S. The estimates range from 50,000 to 100,000. They live for the most part in the slums of large cities, though some travel across the U.S. and into Canada and Mexico as well. Some Gypsies make their living as used-car dealers, others by repairing pots and pans, still others as musicians and dancers. Most are very, very poor.

Because of their lack of political power, the persecution and violence they have encountered both here and abroad has never been adequately recorded. However, it is known that 400,000 Gypsies were murdered in German concentration camps during World War II. Those who survived Buchenwald remember the extraordinary optimism and courage of the Gypsies at the camp in the face of hideous adversity. It is interesting to note that throughout history, Gypsies have reacted with little outward bitterness to hate and persecution. They have avoided organised retaliation and have withdrawn into their own intimate and secret groups, refusing as far as possible to have any contact with the non-Gypsy.

The stereotype of the "thieving, lying" Gypsy has been perpetuated by people who are suspicious of those who are essentially different from them. Jan Yoors, in his vivid, personal account of Gypsy life (*The Gypsies,* Allen & Unwin, 1967), says: "By force of adverse circumstances some Gypsies are forced to practice subsistence thieving — that is, taking their minimal daily needs from the land or its lawful owners: grass for their horses, firewood, potatoes, vegetables or fruit, and of course, the proverbial stray chicken... As with all legends, that of the Gypsies as thieves has been exaggerated. If they were guilty of all the thefts blamed on them, they would have to travel with moving vans or settle down under the weight of their possessions."

The Gypsies, written by Bernice Kohn (Bobbs-Merrill, 1971), is a short account (96 pages) written for ten-to-fourteen-year-olds. It briefly discusses Gypsy history, religion,

magic, some myths and legends, and their status today.
Throughout, the author expresses a grudging admiration for
the life style of the Gypsies, though she makes no effort
discourage the sterotype of the Gypsy as a liar and a thief.
She says: "There is no country in the world where Gypsies do
not have the reputation of being thieves who will 'take
anything that.is not nailed down.' They are also regarded as
outrageous liars and swindlers in business dealings."

In addition, she also writes:

> Gypsies have never been famous for observing the law of
> the land — any land. They have been thieves, shoplifters,
> pickpockets, sellers of shoddy goods, swindlers of every
> sort — but hardly ever murderers or criminals of a very
> grievous sort. Their speciality has been petty crime and
> being quick, clever and deft, they are not too often caught.
> As a result, they have been accused not only of the crimes
> they have committed, but of many others as well.
>
> This may have come about because from the moment of
> their appearance in Europe, Gypsies were suspect,
> discriminated against, persecuted, treated as outcasts and
> pariahs. Or was it the other way around? *Were* Gypsies
> treated poorly because they were a strange minority group
> — or was it because they were thieves, shoplifters,
> pickpockets, etc. The case can be argued both ways, and
> we will never know the true answer.

Is it not possible that a young reader might conclude from
the foregoing statement that Gypsies *deserve* to be persecuted?
This is an appalling attitude toward an oppressed minority to
have in a book for children.

Ms. Kohn has included in the back of her book a glossary
of some English and Romany words and a bibliography.
However, she neglects to include another children's book
already published about Gypsies: Katherine Esty's *Gypsies,
Wanderers in Time* (Meredith Press, 1969). Ms. Esty has
written an intelligent, carefully researched book about
Gypsies. She describes their flight from India into Western

77

Europe in the 15th century, early attitudes toward the
nomads, recent research into the Sanskrit origins of the
Romany language, their persecution during World War II,
and the problems they are facing in the 20th century.
Interspersed throughout her book are fascinating profiles of
individuals — the famous Swedish Gypsy, Milos, for example.
Her anecdotes about her personal experiences with Gypsies
both here and abroad add a dimension of compassion and
perception that is not found in Ms. Kohn's book.

The Esty book ends with an eloquent quotation from
Flaubert: "A week ago, I was enraptured by a camp of
Gypsies that stopped at Rouen... They had aroused the hatred
of the bourgeois even though they were harmless as lambs.
This hatred stems from a deep and complex source; it is to be
found in all champions of order. It is the hatred felt for the
bedouin, the heretic, the philosopher, the recluse, the poet,
and it contains elements of fear. I who am always on the side
of minorities, am driven wild by it."

A third book, *Gypsies,* by John Hornby (Oliver & Boyd
1965), 55 pages, for ages eight to twelve, makes almost no
mention of American Gypsies. Instead, Mr. Hornby has
described Gypsy history and customs and has focused upon
their cultural contributions in music, dance and literature. The
author does not deal with the restrictions that modern society
places upon the Gypsy way of life nor does he discuss the
discrimination and other severe social problems still
confronting Gypsies almost everywhere.

After looking at some of the attitudes shown in non-fiction
about Gypsies, it should be pointed out that one of the main
sources of stereotypes is fiction in which Gypsies play
"minor" roles. To take just one example, consider a
children's classic, *The Good Master* (Harrap 1937). This book,
written and illustrated by Kate Seredy (a Newbery award
winner for *The White Stag*), is about a young girl who is sent
by her father to live on her uncle's farm on the great
Hungarian plains. In a chapter titled "Kate and the Gypsies",
a band of Gypsies passes the Nagy farm. Mr. Nagy, Kate's
uncle, warns her: "'I wouldn't be too friendly with them,

Kate. Perhaps they can't really put spells on you, but they're queer, strange folks. People believe they can work magic. But I *know* one thing,' he laughed. 'They certainly can take things *off* you if you don't watch sharply. They steal like magpies.' "

Later, they visit the Gypsy camp:

"When they reached the camp, a swarm of dirty little urchins surrounded them. 'Money. Meester. Give the poor gypsies money!'

"Father took out a handful of small copper coins and threw them into the air. 'Scramble, now,' he laughed. The little gypsies became a writhing, screaming mass of arms and legs, fighting for the coins like wild cats...

"Father was still laughing, as they walked back to the house. 'They're dirty, thieving, irresponsible good-for-nothings, and yet nobody can be really angry with them. I know they would steal the shirt off my back, but what can I do? They're no worse than the jack rabbits in the corn or the sparrows in the wheat.' "

And indeed, true to the image of the Gypsy stereotype, they steal the chickens, kill the Nagys' fattest pig, and kidnap Kate. For a sensitive young reader, Kate's terrifying experience with the Gypsy band is certain to arouse fears and suspicions of all Gypsies, lingering long after the child has forgotten the story of *The Good Master*.

The Five Chinese Brothers: Time to Retire

Albert V. Schwartz

The Five Chinese Brothers (Bodley Head 1961) is one of the most widely circulated children's books in the U.S. Written and illustrated by Claire Huchet Bishop and Kurt Wiese respectively, the book received considerable critical acclaim when it was published in 1938. "A most ingenious tale," wrote *Library Journal*. "[A] picture book as amusing as it is Chinese," stated the New York Public Library's *Children's Books, 1938.* Wrote the *Boston Herald,* "Spinach, chops and junket have been consumed almost painlessly and at gratifying tempo since *The Five Chinese Brothers* came to town... Mrs. Bishop and Mr. Wiese have... evolved a priceless tale of great appeal." The fact that the book is in its 36th American printing testifies to its success in the marketplace.

Although *The Five Chinese Brothers* has been touted as being authentically "Chinese", the fallacy of this notion is revealed when we examine the book in the context of the time when it was written and then compare it to *The Five Little Liu Brothers* by Wang Y-chuan (Foreign Languages Press, Peking, 1960) — which is based on the same Chinese folk legend that apparently inspired Bishop/Wiese.

The Five Chinese Brothers was published at a time when the Chinese Exclusion Act was in effect, but also a time when some sympathy for the Chinese was being generated due to the sufferings being inflicted on China by the invading Japanese. The book seems, then, to have been in part a response to a new, not necessarily negative, interest in China and the Chinese; but, at the same time, it drew upon the period's popular, extremely negative stereotypes of the

Chinese. These stereotypes are reflected in the Kurt Wiese illustrations (Wiese also illustrated *The Story of Ping* and *You Can Write Chinese*), which are typical of the political cartoons found in the jingoistic U.S. press of the 1930's.

First of all, the drawings endorse the idea popular then *and* now, that Asians "all look alike". While it is entirely legitimate for a story to depict five brothers of any nationality as being identical, the Wiese pictures show not only the brothers but all of the characters — brothers, mother, townspeople, judge, etc. — looking exactly alike. Moreover, the characters' appearances are reduced to the common stereotypical denominator of bilious yellow skin, slit and slanted eyes (Asian people's skin is *not* yellow, and their eyes are neither slanted nor slits), pigtails and "coolie clothes". These caricatures were part and parcel of the perception of Asians and their descendants as subhuman creatures, a perception which led members of the white majority to persecute, ridicule, exploit and ostracise Chinese Americans.

The origins of certain details of the stereotypes and their socio-political significance are noteworthy. The pigtail was a humiliating symbol of subjugation forced upon Chinese peasants by the Manchu ruling class. In the United States, during the Manchu reign in China, white Americans often frightened and humiliated Chinese Americans by cutting off their pigtails, knowing that they couldn't return to China, should they want to, without them. (When the Manchus were overthrown in 1911, the Chinese cut off their pigtails as an act of liberation and adopted new hair styles.)

The "coolie clothes" assigned to the book's characters are also associated with subjugation. The term "coolie" was applied to unskilled and underpaid Chinese labourers in the U.S., while their white counterparts were referred to as "workers". The disrespectful "coolie" concept fostered the exploitation of Chinese American workers by bosses and union leaders alike. (Testifying against Chinese American workers in the U.S. Congress, A.F.L. organiser Samuel Gompers stated: "Keep that cheap chink labour out!") By classifying Chinese American workers as coolies, all the rights labour had won could be denied to them.

The Bishop/Wiese book begins:

> Once upon a time there were Five Chinese Brothers and
> they all looked exactly alike... The First Chinese Brother
> could swallow the sea. The Second Chinese Brother had an
> iron neck. The Third Chinese Brother could stretch... his
> legs. The Fourth Chinese Brother could not be burned.
> And the Fifth Chinese Brother could hold his breath
> indefinitely.

The first brother agrees to take a little boy to the seaside on
condition that the boy will obey him. "'Remember,' said the
First Chinese Brother, 'you must obey me promptly.'" The
brother then swallows the sea. But the boy becomes so
engrossed in collecting small treasures from the dry sea bed
that he ignores the brother's command to return to the shore.
Unable to hold the sea in his mouth any longer, the brother
spits it out and the boy drowns.

Without even hearing both sides of the story, a judge, also
dressed in "coolie" cap and pigtail, sentences the brother to
death by beheading. To be "fair", he allows the brother to go
home to say a last goodbye to his mother. The boy tricks the
judge and "justice" by sending in his place the brother with
the "iron neck".

The townspeople (who all look alike — slits for eyes, coolie
caps, yellow skin, etc. and are otherwise a stereotypically
faceless mass) assemble to witness the punishment. Not one of
them comments on whether justice is or is not being done.
When the beheading aborts and the people's thirst for bloody
vengeance is unsatisfied, they cry out for an even more
horrible form of punishment — death by fire. The brother
who cannot be burned then stands in and, of course, survives.
Each time an attempt at execution fails, the townsfolk
demand a new effort. Hence, the "people" are depicted as a
vindictive mob devoid of human compassion. Finally, the
judge declares, "We have tried to get rid of you in every
possible way and somehow it cannot be done. It must be that

you are innocent." What a mockery of justice, and what a cynical estimation of human behaviour!

Condemnation of *The Five Chinese Brothers* for peddling racism and misanthropy invites the charge that a mountain is being made out of a molehill. Why take the book so seriously, one might ask. The book wasn't intended as an historically accurate narrative; it was meant to be humorous and entertaining — a tall tale of sorts. That may well be, but one is hard put to divorce such a book from the tradition of racism which Asians have had to suffer in U.S. society, or from the specific manifestations of that racism which surfaced during the period in which the book was written. The Asian images presented in the book coincide with and strongly reinforce — intentionally or not — the negative perceptions of Asians which have always been and are still operative in western society. (Such perceptions have also informed foreign policy towards Asian nations.) What a shame that a book whose authors have so skilfully employed basic techniques for capturing and holding a young audience, and which is thus quite entertaining, should be so at the expense of a people and their culture.

The continued exposure of young children to the destructive messages of this tale in nurseries, schools and libraries is most regrettable. About a year ago, when I was working in an elementary school, a teacher mentioned *The Five Chinese Brothers* to her class. One of the children put his fingers at the corners of his eyes. He pulled one up, then one down and said, "My mother is Chinese and my father is Japanese." Then he pulled both eyes up and down at the same time and continued, "and I'm a crazy mixed-up kid." In *Race Attitudes in Children* by Bruno Lasker, a child is quoted as saying, "I don't like the Chinese because the looks of the slant eyes give me a chill." Bigoted attitudes toward Asians are inherent not only in illustrations, but in words like "inscrutable", "distrustful", "crafty", "sneaky", "devious", "unfathomable", "backward", "savage", "obsequious", "stoic" and "yellow peril". As long as children are exposed to illustrations which depict Asians with

83

slits for eyes, and as all looking alike, and to covertly racist language, negative feelings are being engendered.

An English edition of *The Five Little Liu Brothers* by Wang Yuchuan was published in Peking in 1960. It and *The Five Chinese Brothers* share two factors in common: in both, the brothers have extraordinary powers, and they outwit their challengers. There, the similarity ends.

The Five Little Liu Brothers begins:

> In olden days, by the side of a big sea there was a little village which was called Liuchiachuang. One year a woman by the name of Liu Ta-niang whǒ lived in this little village gave birth to quintuplets.

Simple as they are, the title and beginning of the Wang story contain important elements which immediately distinguish it from the Bishop/Wiese version. The location of the story and the mother have *names* — an element that is so frequently omitted from stories written by whites about African American, Chicano, Puerto Rican, Native American and Asian American people. The specific identity which a name connotes checks any inclination on the part of the reader to generalise about "those people". We know we are going to read, not about *the* Chinese, but about a particular group of individuals who are Chinese. The name as a cultural indicator has anti-racist implications for us, although the Chinese author probably styled this story this way in order to authenticate it, not to be anti-racist.

Sometimes when a folk tale from another culture is adapted, cultural indicators are removed for the purposes of "clarification". However, this approach is a disservice rather than an aid to readers because it wipes out important information. Readers need not understand every detail to appreciate a story, and one can learn a lot from a story that is replete with information about a culture.

In the Wang story, the fifth brother — named Lao Five — tends sheep. He is nicknamed "The Know-All" because "he can speak the languages of all birds and animals". While he is tending the flock one day, a richly-dressed "big official" and his men, who are on a hunting expedition, approach and prepare to shoot the sheep. Lao Five warns the sheep, as well as other animals in the vicinity, and they flee to a hiding place in the woods. Enraged, the official orders his men to remove Lao Five to the city, where they lock him in a cage with a tiger — expecting that he will be eaten. Instead, Lao Five and the tiger become friends. The story proceeds with new punishments being decreed by the official, and with each brother defying death according to his "special talent". In the end, the official and his men attempt to drown Lao One — of "the big belly" — but are themselves drowned when he drinks up then spits out the sea, thus swamping their boat.

The value and message of the Wang story are altogether different from the U.S. version. The official and his men, symbols of pompous authority, are the villains, and the simple people are in the right. The brothers are on the side of nature, as represented by the various animals, and justice is on the side of the brothers. In fact, all of the characters — human and animal — receive their just (in the real sense) rewards. In contrast to the Bishop/Wiese interpretation, authority figures are not projected as deserving blind obedience; there is no faceless, blood-thirsty mob of townspeople; humane and decent values are not bent out of shape in service to a dubious form of humour, and though the quintuplet brothers look just alike, they and the other characters are not caricatured. Their skin is beige and their eyes are neither slanted nor slits. At the same time, the Wang story is exciting, humorous, well-written and instructive in a positive way.

By comparison with *The Five Little Liu Brothers,* Bishop/Wiese's *The Five Chinese Brothers* is a relic of historical racism which can only do harm to the self-images of Chinese-descended children and harm to non-Chinese children's potential for bias-free thought and behaviour. As a solution to the problem presented by continued use of this tale as an entertainment vehicle and/or "multi-cultural experience" for young children, we urge the following: 1) that the book be studied and analysed in the classroom to foster awareness of racism and its workings, and 2) that some enterprising teacher or librarian-turned-author adapt either *The Five Little Liu Brothers* or *Seven Brothers* in the same dramatic and exciting mode to which *The Five Chinese Brothers* owes its enduring popularity.

Sexism in Children's Books

What are little girls made of?

Attitudes to sex-roles as seen through illustration

Pippi Longstocking:
Astrid Lindgren and
Richard Kennedy

These days, when Mr. Ratigan came home from the
office, he found his children in such high spirits
that he soon gave up trying to keep them quiet.
He gave up his radio too, since it was drowned
out by music and singing. He didn't even dare
mention his slippers which had been washed away
in the flood. But he couldn't quite give up
those delicious and now very rare dinners.
So he decided to take up cooking himself.

WHEN YOU GROW UP

What would you like to be when you are bigger? Would you like to be a good cook like your father? Or would you like to be a doctor or a nurse?

What would you like to be?

policeman

fireman

sailor

nurse

milkman

farmer

doctor

carpenter

musician

cowboy

butcher

dentist

secretary

good cook

54

Richard Scarry series

93

Keywords Reading Scheme 1A
by W. Murray and J.H. Wingfield

He Bear, She Bear
Stan and Jan Berenstain

We bulldoze roads,
we drive cranes,
we drive trucks,
we drive trains.

We can do all these things, you see,
you see,
whether we are he or she.

Approaches to Sex Education

How Babies are made:
Andrew C. Andry, Steven
Schepp and Blake Hampton

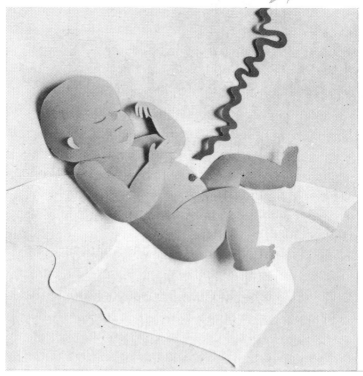

How a Baby is made:
Per Holm Knudsen

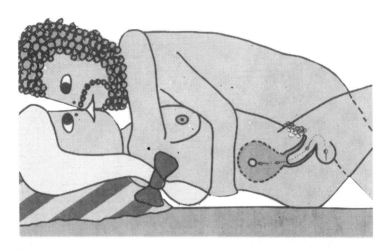

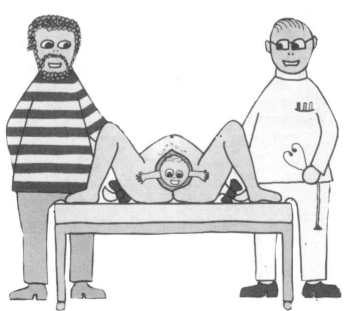

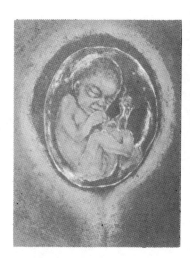

Where do Babies Come from?:
Margaret Sheffield and Sheila
Bewley

Children's Books
From the New China

The cover illustrations seem familiar:
- A 10-year-old boy lies hidden under a bush. On his head is a make-believe helmet made of an old basket. Intently, he spies on an unseen foe.
- A 6-year-old girl in a white smock rides happily on a freshly bandaged wooden horse.
- Two children are busy in a city's streets, bundles of newspapers in their arms.

But in these children's books the subject matter becomes unfamiliar almost as soon as we are past the cover illustrations. The boy in the basket helmet is not spying on imaginary Indians or pirates; he is carefully observing the movements of a very real invading army. The girl on the rocking-horse has not been playing nurse while her brother has the glory of playing doctor. It is she who is the doctor and the wooden horse's leg is really broken. The girl competently uses saw and hammer to repair the break. Nor are the two children with newspapers taking their first step in a Victor Matthews saga of success; they are distributing clandestine papers for a liberation army.

An informal study of 21 children's books produced in China and translated into English (among other languages) by the Foreign Languages Press of Peking reveals several interesting trends and characteristics of children's literature in the People's Republic. A major effort to publish these books in translation has made them widely known in Europe since 1964. At least 180 of these books are known to have been produced before publication was suspended during the Cultural Revolution — a reorientation for which some claim these books must take some credit. But now the Foreign Languages Press in Peking has been releasing them in growing numbers. And finally the English editions have begun slowly to filter into Great Britain and the United States.

Modest production quality is one characteristic of all these books. They are paperbacks, small, often with self-covers of the same stock as the pages. Yet their design, quality of artwork and colour are excellent and the illustrations often shame the glossy, loudly-coloured pictures in Western books. The first impression that these are "cheap" books gives way to an appreciation of their artistic competence. They are proof that books can be inexpensive and still visually attractive.

To readers educated in the Western literary tradition, the characters in these books often appear two-dimensional. The writing style usually seems simplistic. The stories are didactic rather than evocative — at least as far as their verbal content — and to Western taste their messages are so direct as to perhaps be unappealing. However, it would be absurd to assume a cultural *naïveté* on the part of the Chinese people. The style and content of these books can only have been chosen deliberately as a means to achieve a deliberately chosen end. If we would understand today's China, more will be served by examining the values these books promote than by dismissing them as unsophisticated.

Several themes recur in these books, but in most of them only one is central. Stereotyped sex roles are challenged; China's minority peoples (called tribes before the revolution but now referred to as nationalities) are presented; heroes of China's armed struggles are praised; and support of the ideology of the Revolution is preached. Some of these books, particularly those meant to teach moral attitudes to the younger children, are preachy and didactic without apology. It is significant, however, that child characters in these books do not cease to be children even though they are allowed to concern themselves with the same realities as adults.

The traditional oppression of women in pre-revolutionary China has been legendary. In these books the old sex roles are attacked on several levels. In *The Little Doctor,* a book for the very young, it is the girl Ping Ping who is the doctor, treating her little sister's doll, prescribing a good wash for her little brother's Teddy Bear and matter-of-factly using tools (usually reserved for boys) to fix a broken rocking horse. *The Secret Bulletin* is for older children; again it is the girl, Hsiao-fen, who takes charge when she and a boy friend undertake to print and distribute illegal bulletins for the Liberation Army. Hsiao-fen corrects the boy's fumbling attempts to mimeograph the bulletins, shows foresight in ensuring that they have food, and with her quick thinking saves their clandestine mission when the boy's thoughtless bragging almost gets them caught. No children appear in *Red Women's Detachment,* which uses the historical formation of the first Women's Army unit in 1930 to show women as rebels and efficient fighters. In this story one woman joins the army to free herself from a ten-year marriage to a wooden dummy, the effigy of her fiancé who died just before their wedding, which had been forced on her by feudal custom. Interesting, too, is the fact that this book openly recognises that the formation of this first women's detachment — a precedent of great importance from the Chinese political point of view — was done by one of China's minority nationalities, the Li people of Hainan.

Not all of the books in this survey are equally successful in challenging sex roles, however. In *Observation Post 3,* a book for adolescents, a country boy and his sister set out to take a message to the guerrilla fighters during the Japanese occupation. Adult women in the illustrations are always shown engaged in traditional menial household tasks. In the relationship between the boy and the girl it is the boy who is active (he has to win his sister's attention away from the egg she is eating); resourceful (he figures out a way for them to trick a Japanese guard); brave (he continues to lead the way though wounded in the leg); and commanding (he forces his sister to carry on without him). In the final scene — after the mission has been accomplished and, as a consequence, the Japanese have been defeated by the guerrillas — it is the boy who is embraced by the guerrilla chief while his sister looks on from a distance, even though it was she who actually got the message through. It is in this book, too, that racist stereotyping appears. The Japanese soldiers are markedly darker in colour than the Chinese, and they are shown as grotesque caricatures remarkably like the ones in U.S. comic books during World War II.

A little appreciated fact overseas is that approximately six per cent of China's population belong to ethnic or cultural minorities. They are recognised as separate nationalities — 54 in all. Of the 21 books surveyed by the Council, six are about minority nationalities. *Red Women's Detachment* has already been mentioned. *The Horse-Headed Fiddle,* a picture book folk-tale from Inner Mongolia, is a thoroughly charming account of why the Mongolian fiddle is traditionally decorated with the carving of a horse's head. The historic oppression commemorated by the Inner Mongolian people through their folk tale is recognised and preserved in this telling. *Brave Little Shepherd Shaolu* is about a 15-year-old Inner Mongolian shepherd who single-handedly brings a flock of 400 sheep safely through a blizzard. *Hunting With Grandad* depicts the hunting lore of the Olunchun mountain people so sympathetically that any child might well wish to trade places with Nayan, the Olunchun boy. In *Commander Yang's Young Pioneers,* young Koreans join quite naturally with young Chinese to resist the Japanese invasion. *It Happened in a Coconut Grove* is about two Li boys of Hainan Island, in the far south, who cleverly harass a Japanese patrol.

Minority groups are never depicted as "exotic" or alien in these books, although in two *(The Horse-Headed Fiddle* and *Hunting With Grandad)* elements unique to their own national culture are depicted. In the other four books they are shown as participating positively in the issues that affect all of China. Noticeably absent is any expression of paternalism toward the minority nationalities or any implication that they must prove their equality.

The books constantly recall the struggles against the Japanese and against the Kuomintang forces. Not only do those struggles serve as background for some of the stories already mentioned, they are the subjects of two more picture books, both of which are taken from Chinese films. Both

were published after the Cultural Revolution. *Mine Warfare*
(1971) is a photo book about popular resistance to the
Japanese; it centres on the determination and ingenuity of the
people, who find effective ways of combating an organised
army. *Fighting North and South* (1972) tells the story of the
defeat by the People's Liberation Army of Chiang Kai-shek.
In these recent books thematic emphasis is still on the ability
of a united people successfully to pit determination and
ingenuity against a powerful war machine.

A somewhat different approach to developing a
commitment to armed struggle among Chinese children
underlies three of the books. *Huang Chi-kuang, Immortal
Hero Yang Ken-sze* and *Stories from Liu Hu-lan's
Childhood* provide individual models of heroism. The last is
for quite young readers and contains four very moralistic
stories of incidents from the childhood (she was killed by the
Kuomintang forces at 15) of Liu Hu-lan. The
titles suggest the nature of the stories: "Sisterly Love",
"Protecting the Poor Children", "Helping to Catch Spies"
and "Sending Eggs" (to a wounded soldier of the Liberation
Army). *Huang Chi-kuang* is for older readers. The hero was
born in a poor family in a remote province and grew up to
volunteer to fight in the Korean War, where he died as a
hero, flinging himself single-handed against an enemy machine
gun. The story ends with a flourish typical of these books:
"News of Huang's heroic deed immediately spread
throughout the country serving as a glorious example to
China's soldiers and citizens. His noble image shall always
remain in the hearts of the Chinese people." *Immortal Hero
Yang Ken-sze* fought the Japanese, then the Kuomintang and
finally died as the last man defending a hill in Korea, where a
monument to his memory now stands. In this book for older
children the horrors of pre-revolutionary China are more fully
portrayed, as are the political development and commitment
of the hero. All three heroes are of the people and are
committed to selfless service for the revolution. A picture of
the values that China wants its children to respect and to
develop shows through these books clearly.

Chinese children's books are available from: Guanghwa Company, 9 Newport Place, London WC2.

Enid Blyton's Girls

from *You're a Brick, Angela!*

Mary Cadogan and Patricia Craig

Enid Blyton's conventionality is nowhere more clearly
apparent than in the distinctions which she makes in her
treatment of boy and girl characters. Her boys are consistently
"chivalrous" in the most rigid way:

> "I'm not taking the girls," said Jack, firmly. "I don't
> mind any risk myself — but I won't risk anything with the
> girls. You can come, of course, Philip."

> "Well, decent boys like looking after their girl cousins or
> sisters," said Julian. "And oddly enough decent girls like
> it..."

> The girls cried bitterly at this. They thought it was very
> unfair. They couldn't know that Andy didn't feel at all
> certain of ever getting home, and was very much afraid of
> the girls being washed overboard when big waves came. He
> and Tom were strong — and besides they were boys — but
> the girls would never be able to stand tossing about on a
> raft for days and days.

Only in George of the Famous Five are the girl's instinct for
self-assertion and her demand for equality adumbrated. The
author has withheld complete approval from George, and for
this reason George is one of her most interesting creations. It
is the characters of whom she approves most who are the
nonentities — Julian, Dick, Jack, Larry, Roger, Peter. George
is not quite fairly treated: there is no suggestion that her
fantasy of being a boy is just as "normal" as Anne's

acceptance of a "housewifely" rôle. Her cousins go along with George's eccentric behaviour for the sake of peace, and because they like her: along with the "masculine" qualities of recklessness and aggression she has cultivated those of loyalty, courage ("You're the bravest girl I know") and truthfulness. In *Five Go To Mystery Moor* (1954) George is brought face to face with another girl who behaves as she does; for comic effect the author has to make them dislike one another on sight:

> "...That awful girl Henrietta too. Why do we have to put up with her?"
> "Oh — Henry!" said Anne, with a laugh. "I should have thought you'd find a lot in common with another girl like yourself, who would rather be a boy, and tries to act like one!"

George and Henry react to one another "like a couple of idiotic school*girls*", and this makes George's well-adjusted cousins laugh. It also underlines that fact that they are *not* boys, and Henry herself is forced in the end to accept this fact, with its more hateful implications. When she is at a loss to know what to do, she thinks, "... there's no grown-up here tonight except Mrs Johnson... I'm going to dress, and then get William. He's only eleven, I know, but he's very sensible, and he's a boy. He'll know what to do. I only *pretend* to be a boy." This, one feels, is the author's view of girls who "pretend to be boys": that they are pretentious and silly. They will "grow out" of it; the growing out is a process of adjustment. "Real" boys who are forced to take notice of the trait are inclined to sound dismissive, smug and obtuse: this is in spite of the author who plainly felt that she was giving the reasonable, balanced view: " 'Hold your horses, George, old thing,' said Julian, surprised. 'After all, you've often been pleased when people have taken *you* for a boy, though goodness knows why. I thought you'd grown out of it a bit...' "

George is "difficult", but her quirks, her originality, are

excusable because of her age. Grown-up female characters in the books who do not conform to the traditional, cosy image of "a mother" are made out to be utterly shallow and worthless. The two types — maternal and worldly — are contrasted most explicitly in *Six Cousins at Mistletoe Farm* (1948): the "hard-working, cheerful, sensible" farmer's wife, and the spoilt, high-heeled, whining, vanity-ridden "Aunt Rose". Aunt Rose is "brought to her senses" only when she is faced with the prospect of losing her husband and children; she resolves to subjugate her own interests and inclinations to theirs, thereby fitting in with a pattern of self-effacing domesticity which the author considered admirable.

Her recurrent use of the "happy family" as a fictional motif has a direct relation to her own experience. Her adolescence was insecure; she disliked her mother, whom she saw for the last time in the 1920s (Mrs Theresa Blyton died in 1950). The author's father walked out on his wife and children in 1912, the episode was re-created nearly 40 years later, in *Six Bad Boys*. This is perhaps Enid Blyton's nastiest story; she has taken, unusually, a "topical" theme and sentimentalised it, bringing to the problem of juvenile delinquency an attitude dispiritingly retrogressive. Of the six boys, four are unredeemably lower class, outside the author's pale; the two whose "downfall" is related have problem families, we are told that they are good boys at heart but emotionally deprived. The father of one has deserted his family, driven away by his wife's querulousness; the other boy's mother wilfully creates the vacuum in her son's conscience by her decision to *go out to work*. At the time, in the early '50s, there was a great deal of public concern about latch-key children and the morally deteriorating effect on a child of coming into an empty house. A mother's place quite literally was in the home; she could leave it only at the expense of her children's ethical well-being. Of course Enid Blyton's own childhood experiences had predisposed her to accept this debatable view; it is stated over and over again in *Six Bad Boys.* Having got hold of what she believed to be a serious, psychological truth the author could not leave it alone. The pathetic "bad boys" find a way into the cellar of an empty house; they try to manufacture in this dismal setting a measure of the home comforts which they all lack. By this simple device the author emphasises the nature of their moral deficiencies. Of course they have to steal money to "furnish" the place. They are caught, brought up in court, and some are sent to approved schools. Enid Blyton's ultimate remedies, however, are as weak, exasperating and implausible as her causes: "Coo — I shan't be bad again, now I've got a proper home!" The diminishment of "badness", the banality, the whole cotton-wool lack of sharpness or insight are typical of the author at her worst. Here, she has subordinated characterisation entirely to an endorsement of her own point of view. The book is an addition to the anti-feminist propaganda of the time. This was compounded largely of the findings of popularised anthropological and psychological studies. Women's "natural" functions naturally were stressed, and the gloss was in the lipstick, shining kitchen equipment, the bright magazines whose golden girl typically renounced her birthright for a home in the suburbs.

The guilt which society imposed on working mothers is likely to have had an effect more psychologically damaging to their children than the mere fact of a temporarily empty house. The "villain" of *Six Bad Boys* is Bob's widowed mother, who insists on her right to work: 12-year-old Bob, however, expects her to sit at home all day keeping the house warm for him:

"I think I shall soon find a job to do," said his mother. "I'm bored now. And I want a bit more money."

"Don't do that," said Bob, suddenly filled with panic, though he didn't know why. "I like to think of you at home all day. I don't want to think of an empty house — and no fire — and no kettle boiling. Don't you get a job, Mum..."

Enid Blyton's poor, ill-treated Bob in fact is self-pitying, destructive, a thoroughly unsympathetic emotional blackmailer. His whining has a solid, socially-approved backing, however: "'He is your only child,' (said the magistrate) 'Don't you think you could give up your work and care for him again?'" Few mothers in that situation would have the gumption to answer No, as Bob's mother does; this is presented as the final evidence of the unfortunate woman's hard-heartedness. The story has a happy ending, of course: Bob is adopted by the "proper" family next door: "'I used to envy them because I hadn't a family too,' he thought. 'But now it's *my* family... I belong! Here I go walking in, to join my family!'"

It is odd that the need to be employed, usually so serious, dignified or forceful a topic, should be made here to seem frivolous, indicating in its subject a flighty nature. But it is not grim financial necessity which drives Bob's mother out of the house but boredom: the point seems to be that it is morally justifiable for mothers to be employed only if they would *prefer* to be at home. However it is looked at, the tedious, restrictive concept of "women's work" was always basically illogical...

Pippi Longstocking — A Feminist or Anti-Feminist Work?

Kik Reeder

One of the most popular heroines in juvenile literature is a 9-year-old red-haired, pigtailed girl called Pippi Longstocking who lives alone with a small monkey and a big horse and does what she darn well pleases. And considering that she has been around for over thirty years (Astrid Lindgren began *Pippi Longstocking* in March, 1944), it is safe to say that she is well on her way to becoming a classic.

When Pippi first appeared in her own country (Sweden), she was an instant success, because she fundamentally broke the pattern of what up till then had been the accepted formula for little girl heroines. Things don't happen to Pippi — she *makes* them happen. She is self-assertive, inventive and independent with lots of charm and imagination. She lives alone in her own house, her mother having conveniently died when she was very little, and her father, a sea captain, having been blown overboard on one of his many voyages.

But Pippi is no Little Orphan Annie. She loves every minute of her freedom and independence. There is no one to tell her when to go to bed, she can eat cream cake for breakfast if she pleases, she doesn't bother with housecleaning or other dull chores, unless she can make a game out of them. In fact she doesn't have to put up with any of the dreary demands that are made on most children. She dresses with a happy disregard for convention and especially favours one brown and one black stocking and a pair of enormous black shoes. Should the mood hit her, Pippi puts on ghastly make-up or picks her nose at parties.

She also happens to be the strongest girl in the world (she

can lift a horse without the slightest effort) *and* she is rich as can be. So when she can't argue her way out of a situation — which she does very well, by the way — she simply resorts to force and removes any undesirables, be they policemen, social workers, burglars or circus managers. And whatever she needs in the world she can buy. Needless to say, Pippi sees no reason to go to school and she treats all adults with total lack of respect. (As a matter of fact doubts have been raised in Sweden as to this image of adults as total fools, or threatening old people, in the Pippi books. If the adult world, and not just authority, but all adults, are made to look entirely foolish and/or threatening, unkind and full of ill will, what then are children to expect of themselves as adults?)

Anyway it no wonder Pippi Longstocking is popular with her young readers! She personifies the most cherished and secret dream of any child — that of being omnipotent and able to function without any interference from the adult world. Independent and disobedient children are not uncommon in children's literature, but they are seldom girls. And Pippi is super girl, tomboy, feminist or plain horror, all wrapped into one delicious creature, as popular with English children as she is with Swedish ones. She is "... a children's safety valve against the pressure of authority and daily life: This is the secret of [her] incredible success." *(The Horn Book Magazine,* February, 1973).

Yet, *Pippi Longstocking* (and the two other books in the series, *Pippi Goes Aboard* and *Pippi in the South Seas)* has recently come under mounting criticism in her home country, Sweden. For although Pippi herself is a bit too "unreal" to truly identify with, she inhabits a world which is very real indeed, a world which most *white* children of any nationality can recognise very easily. It is a world filled with overt racism and hidden sexism, very much in the Western tradition of children's literature.

As it happens, Pippi's father, the sea captain who fell overboard, didn't drown after all. He just floated ashore and landed on a *cannibal* island, where he instantly was made a cannibal king, something Pippi considers very "stylish".

113

Why a cannibal island of all things? They were pretty few and far between by 1944. Well, because cannibals by tradition are thought of as hilariously funny, savage and adoring of whites. Pippi herself can't wait for her father to come and get her, so that she in turn can become a "cannibal Princess". And when father and daughter actually arrive in the Canny Cannibal Island *(Pippi in the South Seas)* the inhabitants are duly overcome by awe:

The crowd surged forward when the gangplank was lowered. Shouts of 'Ussamkuru, kussomkare' were heard, which meant: 'welcome back, fat white chief!'

And when Pippi's father mounts his throne to do a bit of ruling over his faithful people, he no longer wears ordinary clothes, but dresses in "royal attire, with a crown on his head, a straw skirt around his waist, a necklace of shark's teeth round his neck, and thick rings round his ankles".

There is a very condescending attitude towards language as well as dress. "Luckily Captain Longstocking had been on the island for so long that some of the Canny Cannibals had learnt a little of his language." (Heaven forbid that he should learn any of theirs!) "Of course they did not know the meaning of difficult words like 'postal order' and 'Major-General' but they had picked up quite a lot just the same." (The poor, pitiful ignoramuses!)

Although the Canny Cannibal children have lived on the island all their lives, it takes a white girl to save them from sharks and outsmart a couple of bandits who wish to steal their pearls.

Now, in all fairness to Astrid Lindgren, it can be argued that Pippi is always the leader and the solver of all problems, but the picture that is painted of the smiling, dancing, docile and incompetent "cannibals" is too much the traditional, stereotyped image of Third World people to stand unchallenged. There is nothing in the depiction of the "natives" that in any way adds to the story; they are what they are, incapable of ruling themselves simply because they are "natives". It takes a white man to set things straight. It is the old colonial thinking all over again and it is strongly felt by certain Swedes that such outmoded themes ought to be deleted from any children's book, and especially one with such impact on young minds as the bestselling *Pippi Longstocking*.

In the United States Pippi has been hailed as the first feminist children's book. *Ms.* magazine recently (January, 1974) called her "one of the most independent and inspiring female characters in children's literature".

Independent — yes. Inspiring — possibly. But female — hardly. In the recommended list of juvenile books that the New York City Public Library puts out she is referred to as a tomboy. The "nice" people in the tiny Swedish town where Pippi resides consider her a horror. And to her best friends, Tommy and Annika, she is simply more fun than anybody else. Pippi is not a "real" girl at all; she is made of the same stuff as Peter Pan and other "invisible" playmates we've all read about and loved as children, larger than life and capable of all the things "normal" children can only dream about.

It is soon apparent that Pippi isn't a girl at all, even a tomboy, but a boy in disguise. Astrid Lindgren has simply equipped Pippi with all the traits we have come to think of as male. She never cries; she is aggressive and unafraid, she has a monkey and a horse for pets but doesn't even own a doll, she stands up to all authority and she wants to be a pirate when she grows up. She is extremely generous with gifts and parties but when necessary she can dole out punishment to a bunch of bullies. In other words, Pippi acts like a "real" man.

In contrast, Pippi's friends Tommy and Annika are perfectly "normal". They have a mother and a father. They are obedient and well-behaved children who always do what they are told. Annika never dirties her clothes and Tommy never bites his nails. Tommy is a "real" boy, always ready to follow Pippi's suggestions, no matter how daring, and Annika is a "real" girl, always a little hesitant and scared at first when Pippi and Tommy play rough. She needs a bit of prompting before she can overcome her "natural" shyness, she cries easily and is forever following the others around like a shadow.

But most baffling of all is the fact that the supposedly liberated Pippi is herself full of sexist attitudes toward her two friends. At the end of the first chapter in *Pippi Longstocking,* Pippi gives each of her new playmates little gifts to remember her by. "Tommy's was a knife with a gleaming mother-of-pearl handle, and Annika's a little box decorated on the lid with pieces of shell. In the box there was a ring with a green stone." And when Pippi on one occasion hides things for her friends to find, it is a useful item for Tommy (a notebook with a silver pencil) but for Annika a red coral necklace. Tommy also gets a flute, some paint and a jeep, while Annika gets more things to adorn herself with, a brooch and a red sunshade.

The sex roles are so clearly defined that although Pippi herself doesn't play with dolls, she doesn't think twice before buying one for Annika (*Pippi Goes Aboard*) and for Tommy — guess what? An air gun! And when Tommy decides that he too wants to become a pirate like Pippi when he grows up, Annika is very upset and says: "I'm afraid to be a pirate. What shall *I* do?" But Pippi knows. "Oh, you can come all the same," she says, *"to dust the pianola"*. (Italics mine.)

Even when dealing with Pippi's absent mother and father, the writer manages a nice bit of sexism. The mother is whisked off to heaven, where she is now an angel, watching over Pippi, while the father "formerly the terror of the seas, [is] now Cannibal King". What can be more passive and spiritless(!) than an angel? What more fascinating and awe-inspiring than a father who is a terror?

Once again, just as with racism, the sexism serves no purpose other than to perpetuate well established sex roles without questioning, without evaluation. Pippi embodies a complete set of glorified but questionable white, male values: strength, wealth, success, defiance and staunch unemotionalism. Feminists in both America and Sweden are beginning to feel that there are a great many so-called female values that need appreciation as well. Tenderness, consideration for others, and richness of feeling ought no longer to be demerited as "silly" and "feminine" but elevated as most desirable attributes in both sexes.

That Lindgren has also created once of the most amazing, hilarious and charming heroines in juvenile literature doesn't alter any of this. On the contrary, the mere fact that Pippi is increasingly successful (see below) among young readers, makes it more important than ever that parents, teachers, librarians and publishers are made aware of these negative aspects of the books. Now, when the concepts of racism and sexism are under mounting scrutiny all over the world, a revision of the Pippi books would seem both necessary and timely. For although this is neither the place nor the time to worry about Pippi's economic future, both Astrid Lindgren and her publishers might soon find that their little gold mine has become obsolete.

And that would ultimately deprive countless youngsters all over the world of one of their most rewarding reading experiences. The Pippi books would be just as funny, just as "inspiring", without their racist and sexist aspects. As Pippi herself says: "Don't worry about me. I'll always come out on top."

Pippi Longstocking has been translated into more than 20 languages, including Bulgarian, Danish, Estonian, English, Finnish, French, Hebrew, Dutch, Icelandic, Italian, Japanese, Norwegian, Polish, Portuguese, Russian (in which she is extremely popular), Serbo-Croatian, Slovakian, Slovenian, Spanish, Swahili, and German; and Persian and Singhalese editions are now in preparation. More than 4,500,000 copies have been sold in the U.S. alone and 50,000,000 have been sold worldwide.

Uncle, Buy Me a Contraceptive...

Ariel Dorfman and Armand Mattelart

This extract comes from **How to Read Donald Duck,**
*a provocative critique of the imperialist content in the Disney
family of comics. The book first appeared in Chile in 1971,
but since the Pinochet coup it has been banned and burned
there. An English language edition is available from
International General. The book's authors point out how the
Disney comics — which vary in story-line and emphasis from
country to country — contain beneath their blandly innocent
surface a potent ideological message. Here Dorfman and
Mattelart analyse the position of females and the aberrant
family and sexual structure of the Disney world.*

There is one basic product which is never stocked in the
Disney store: parents. Disney's is a universe of uncles and
grand-uncles, nephews and cousins; the male-female
relationship is that of eternal fiancés. Scrooge McDuck is
Donald's uncle, Grandma Duck is Donald's aunt (but not
Scrooge's wife), and Donald is the uncle of Huey, Dewey, and
Louie. Cousin Gladstone Gander is a "distant nephew" of
Scrooge; he has a nephew of his own called Shamrock, who
has two female cousins. Then there are the more distant
ancestors like grand-uncle Swashbuckle Duck, and Asa Duck,
the great-great-great uncle of Grandma Duck; and (most
distant of all) Don de Pato, who was associated with the
Spanish Armada. The various cousins include Gus Goose,
Grandma Duck's idle farmhand, Moby Duck the sailor, and
an exotic oriental branch with a Sheik and Mazuma Duck,
"the richest bird in South Afduckstan", with nephews. The
genealogy is tipped decisively in favour of the masculine

sector. The ladies are spinsters, with the sole exception of Grandma Duck who is apparently widowed without her husband having died, since he appears just once under the suggestive title "History Repeats Itself". There are also the cow Clarabelle (with a short-lived cousin), the hen Clara Cluck, the witch Magica de Spell, and naturally Minnie and Daisy, who, being the girl friends of the most important characters are accompanied by nieces of their own (Daisy's are called April, May, and June; she also has an uncle of her own, Uncle Dourduck, and Aunts Drusilla and Tizzy).

Since these women are not very susceptible to men or matrimonial bonds, the masculine sector is necessarily and perpetually composed of bachelors accompanied by nephews, who come and go. Mickey has Morty and Ferdy, Goofy has Gilbert (and an uncle "Tribilio"), and Gyro Gearloose has Newton; even the Beagle Boys have uncles, aunts and nephews called the Beagle Brats (whose female cousins, the Beagle Babes, make the occasional appearance). It is predictable that any future demographic increase will have to be the result of extra-sexual factors.

Even more remarkable is the duplication — and triplication — in the baby department. There are four sets of triplets in this world: the nephews of Donald and the Beagle Boys, the nieces of Daisy, and the inevitable three piglets.

The quantity of twins is greater still. Mickey's nephews are an example, but the majority proliferate without attribution to any uncle: the chipmunks Chip and Dale, the mice Gus and Jaq. This is all the more significant in that there are innumerable other examples outside of Disney: Porky and Petunia and nephews; Woody Woodpecker and nephews; and the little pair of mice confronting the cat Tom.

... In this bleak world of family clans and solitary pairs, subject to the archaic prohibition of marriage within the tribe, and where each and every one has his own mortgaged house but never a home, the last vestige of parenthood, male or female, has been eliminated.

The advocates of Disney manage a hasty rationalisation of these features into proof of innocence, chastity and proper restraint. Without resorting polemically to a thesis on infant sexual education already outmoded in the nineteenth century, and more suited to monastic cave dwellers than civilised people, it is evident that the absence of father and mother is not a matter of chance. One is forced to the paradoxical conclusion that in order to conceal normal sexuality from children, it is necessary to construct an aberrant world — one which, moreover, is suggestive of sexual games and innuendo. One may wrack one's brains trying to figure out the educational value of so many uncles and cousins; presumably they help eradicate the wicked taint of infant sexuality.

... There is one sector of Disney society which is beyond the reach of criticism: the female. As in the male sector, the lineage also tends to be avuncular, except that the woman has no chance of switching roles in the dominator-dominated relationship. Indeed, she is never challenged because she plays her role to perfection, whether it be humble servant or constantly courted beauty queen; in either case, subordinate to the male. Her only power is the traditional one of seductress, which she exercises in the form of coquetry. She is denied any further role which might transcend her passive, domestic nature. There are women who contravene the "feminine code", but they are allied with the powers of darkness. The witch, Magica de Spell is a typical antagonist, but not even she abandons aspirations proper to her "feminine" nature. Women are left with only two alternatives (which are not really alternatives at all): to be Snow White or the Witch, the little girl housekeeper or the wicked stepmother. Her brew is of two kinds: the homely stew and the dreadful magic poison. And since she is always cooking for the male, her aim in life is to catch him by one brew or the other.

If you are no witch, don't worry ma'am: you can always keep busy with "feminine" occupations; dressmaker, secretary, interior decorator, nurse, florist, cosmetician, or air hostess. And if work is not your style, you can always become president of the local charity club. In all events, you can always fall back upon eternal coquetry — this is your common denominator, even with Grandma Duck and Madame Mim.

In his graphic visualisation of these coquettes Disney resorts constantly to the Hollywood actress stereotype. Although they are sometimes heavily satirised, they remain a single archetype with their physical existence limited to the escape-hatch of amorous struggle (Disney reinforces the stereotype in his famous films for "the young" as for example, the fairies in *Pinocchio* and *Peter Pan*). Disney's moral stand as to the nature of this struggle is clearly stated, in a scene like the one where Daisy embodies infantile, Doris Day-style qualities against the Italianate vampiress Silvia.

Man is afraid of this kind of woman (who wouldn't be?). He eternally and fruitlessly courts her, takes her out, competes for her, wants to rescue her, showers her with gifts. Just as the troubadours of courtly love were not permitted carnal contact with the women of their lords, so these eunuchs live in an eternal foreplay with their impossible virgins. Since they can never fully possess them, they are in constant fear of losing them. It is the compulsion of eternal frustration, of pleasure postponed for better domination. Woman's only retreat in a world where physical adventure, criticism and even motherhood has been denied her, is into her own sterile sexuality. She cannot even enjoy the humble domestic pleasures permitted to real-life women, as enslaved as they are — looking after a home and children. She is perpetually and uselessly waiting around, or running after some masculine idol, dazzled by the hope of finding at last a true man. Her only *raison d'etre* is to become a sexual object, infinitely solicited and postponed. She is frozen on the threshold of satisfaction and repression among impotent people. She is denied pleasure, love, children, communication. She lives in a centripetal, introverted, egolatrous world; a parody of the island-individual. Her condition is solitude, which she can never recognise as such. The moment she questions her role, she will be struck from the cast of characters.

Mr Worm or Mr Men?

An examination of the *Mr Men* books

Judith Stinton

The Mr Men books are everywhere. You may not have heard
of them, but look around and you'll see them, quietly
spawning in every bookshop, newsagent, supermarket or
village post office. And they are not alone. They bring all
their accessories with them: Mr Men mugs, Mr Men colouring
books, table mats, jigsaw puzzles, yoghurts and eggcups. Ask
any child and she'll tell you, she may even have one in her
pocket, for they are pocket-size books with colourful shiny
covers, each one the story of a different Mr Man.

They are simple stories, simply told. Each figure represents
a different characteristic, mental, moral or physical (Mr
Daydream, Mr Lazy, Mr Small). They are illustrated by
equally simple drawings in primary colours which aspire to the
level of a two year old — arms sticking out from round faces,
often no nose or ears. They live in two-dimensional houses
surrounded by jelly-like clouds and stilted flowers. The
drawings are those of a rather charmless Dick Bruna. They are
easily recognisable and children like to collect them. As with
the Ladybird series, they feel they are "their books".

Early examples of the series are Mr Happy and Mr Tickle.
They are rather more endearing than later characters. Mr
Happy is "fat, round, and happy!" and lives in Happyland.
He descends upon Mr Miserable who is anxious to change his
state.

"'I'd give anything to be happy' said Mr Miserable. 'But
I'm so miserable I don't think I could ever be happy' he
added, miserably."

Mr Happy teaches him to smile and finally to laugh. Then the moral is drawn.

Mr Tickle too makes people laugh. He has "extraordinary long arms" which can reach out to tickle while he remains hidden. He causes chaos wherever he goes: uproar in the classroom, traffic jams, apples all over the shop. His octopus tentacles are obviously amusing to children but, oddly, there's no moral here about the dangers of disruption or of undermining a teacher's authority. Mr Tickle continues to tickle.

Other characters do learn their lesson. *Mr Uppity* is a comedy of manners. Mr Uppity wears a monocle on his puce, snooty face and a tall top hat. He lives in Big Town. (There are often echoes of Enid Blyton's Noddy books in these stories. Places have baby names and episodes are recounted in a bright, coy voice. Mr Uppity encounters a goblin who "skipped off the way goblins do". The goblin, like Big Ears in the Noddy books, has had his sting removed.) Later, with the help of a little magic, Mr Uppity learns that politeness pays.

The magic word used by the goblin in this story is "wobblygobblygook". That unenchanting expression is a typical example of the low imaginative level of the series. Mr Lazy lives in Yawn Cottage, Sleepyland. Mr Skinny visits Dr Plump in Fatland. When human figures are introduced they have stock names out of Happy Families — Mr Meat the butcher, Mrs Crumb the baker's wife, Mr Bowler the hatter. Having established a formula for the books their author, Roger Hargreaves, continues to use it through almost forty stories with hardly any variation. A story will open with a picture of the character's house, followed by an account of his amazing funniness, meanness, immense height or whatever, followed by a description of how or what he eats for breakfast, followed by a series of encounters with cardboard shopkeepers followed by an ending in which he may or may not learn his lesson. Thin as they appear, the stories are padded out with rather laboured repetition:

" 'What was that?' shrieked Mr Jelly. 'It's a lion! I heard it

growl! Oh goodness gracious! Oh dear me! A lion! A huge
lion with enormous teeth! A huge lion with enormous teeth
that's going to bite me in two! A huge ferocious lion with
enormous sharp teeth that's going to bite me in two if not
three!'" (Note, too, the overgenerous use of exclamation
marks.)

Children often find such outbursts funny. To an adult eye,
the visual jokes are more successful, for example Mr Topsy-
Turvy's clock which runs the wrong way round. (Variations of
this idea recur: Mr Lazy's clock shows only four hours.
"Everything takes so long to do there's only time for four
hours a day!")

There are other similarities in the stories. Mr Topsy-Turvy
causes disruption in the same way as Mr Tickle, creating
traffic jams and general chaos. Mr Quiet's story is the obverse
of Mr Noisy's. Mr Nonsense is described as a friend of Mr
Silly, but seems more like an identical twin.

An interesting exception is Mr Daydream, who takes a little
boy called Jack on a dream journey. They fly to Africa and
land in a jungle. "It was very hot!" An elephant picks Jack
up in his trunk: "It was very high!" and a crocodile takes
them across the river. "It was very helpful!" To escape the
crocodile's eventual trap Mr Daydream transports Jack to
Australia where he learns to throw a boomerang. Such
stereotyped adventures make the conclusion that
"daydreaming is more fun than history!" rather unlikely.

This kind of conclusion is characteristic of Mr Hargreaves.
A steady anti-intellectual strain can be felt throughout the
series. Libraries are places where you have to whisper *(Mr
Quiet)*. Mr Clever turns out to be extremely stupid. Everyone
wears spectacles in Cleverland where he lives. Even the worm
who pops up so frequently has turned into a swot. Doctors
and teachers are also bespectacled and sadly ineffectual with
it. Mr Impossible, Mr Topsy-Turvy and Mr Daydream all visit
and upset classrooms of children. Dr Makeyouwell cannot
solve Mr Bounce's problem. Dr Plump fails with Mr Skinny.
He prescribes a large cream cake, half a dozen doughnuts and
twelve currant buns but ends up swallowing his own medicine.

(Mr Greedy then takes over and tutors Mr Skinny until he develops a pot-belly.)

A character who has been helped or learnt his lesson by the end of one story may reappear in another having reverted to type. Mr Jelly has begun quaking with fear again when he reappears in *Mr Clever.* The characters are like members of a select club, treated like old friends when they crop up in other stories. This could be quite a part of their appeal to children, along with the pocket size, the undemanding text and illustrations and the silly repetitious jokes.

The Mr Men, instead of being doubly male as their name might suggest, are curiously sexless. In fact they show no more signs of gender than the ever-observing worm. They are isolated figures, passing in and out of other lives without real contact or warmth. The human figures who make brief, background appearances are classified by trade or profession. Mr Brick is a builder, Mrs Scrub works at the laundry. Mrs Crumb is the baker's wife. As might be expected, they stick without exception to their roles: they are labelled by their jobs alone in a mundanely predictable pack. They too are isolated. William, the little boy in *Mr Impossible,* has a pair of placid parents, but they make only a short appearance. William is lucky to have them at all — and particularly his mother. There are few female figures in the series and none of them is of much importance to a story. The books are written almost entirely from a male viewpoint, that of a club armchair, where women are a half-forgotten species.

Even Mr Hargreaves seems finally to have realised the limitations. He has recently begun a new set of tales about "sort of" animals who live in a land called Timbuctoo. They follow much the same formula as the Mr Men books, and the characters show about as much resemblance to real animals as the Mr Men do to people. Mr Hargreaves has moved on, but he has not moved very far.

D Is for Dictionary
S Is for Stereotyping

Barbara A. Schram

Being aware of the sex and race role stereotyping that is
rampant in children's story books and text books, I find
myself carefully "checking out" each new book before I give
it to a child. I'm always surprised and delighted when I find
one that is a rare exception to the usual vicious pattern. I was
not prepared, however, for the magnitude of stereotyping I
uncovered when "checking out" children's dictionaries. While
story books are after all, only fabrications of someone's
imagination, dictionaries, so I thought, were filled with *facts,*
objective *truths.*

After carefully reading through the dictionaries, ranging
from those intended for under fives to those suggested for
secondary use, I discovered that words can be defined in such
a way that what might seem like *facts* and *truth* are really the
opinion and *bias* of the editors. I also found an article
describing a large-sample, computerised study conducted by
lexicographers of a major publishing company reached the
same conclusions as did my less rigorous research using all the
children's dictionaries on the shelf of a central Manhattan
public library.

I examined these dictionaries primarily to see how sexist
they were. I did not concentrate on their racism, but it must
be said that the dictionaries are, in general, racist by omission
if not by commission.

For example, black and other Third World people are
rarely included in the illustrations, especially in the older
books. When minorities *are* shown, they serve mainly as
"props" for "exotic" dress — for parkas (Eskimos), saris
(Indian women), burnouses (Arabs), and the like. The most
recent dictionaries have of course begun to make an effort to

include minorities in all types of illustrations — but there is still a long way to go.

I would also add that, in not focusing on the racism in dictionaries, I did not seek to document the value structure built into the use of the words "white" and "black". I did not count the number of positive synonyms or connotations associated with "black". However, a quick look at the words paired with white — pure, innocent, etc. — and those matched with black — evil, gloomy, etc. — will reveal to the most casual reader what is wrong.

These are my findings from two solid days of reading children's dictionaries, days filled with eyestrain, boredom and outrage.

1. Editors of dictionaries, especially of those written for very young children, are uncreative copycats.

While the definition of a word — *hit*, for example — cannot vary dramatically from one dictionary to the next, there is no reason why the sentence used to help children place the word in its logical context can not vary a lot. Yet, in three picture dictionaries, I read:

John *hit* the ball.
Tom will *hit* the ball with his tennis racket.
The boy will *hit* the ball with his bat.

When they put the word *strong* into a sentence, I read:

The *strong* man lifts the weights.
The man is *strong*. He can lift heavy weights.
A *strong* man can lift heavy things.

These and countless other such "stimulating" sentences — obviously paraphrased from one book to the next — lead me to believe that new picture dictionaries are written with scissors and tape. Thus, whatever inanities and biases exist in one dictionary are mirrored and thus perpetuated in each subsequent "new" book or "revised" edition. Comparing each of the books' entries for several different words led me inevitably to my next conclusion.

2. In dictionaries, just as in the rest of the world of children's books, females (and of course Third World people as well) are virtually invisible. This holds true for most of the dictionaries I read, but the picture dictionaries are the worst offenders.

In their dull simplicity and their underestimation of the intelligence of children, the dictionaries almost always use a pronoun or person's name in each sentence. Thus it is always *John, Tom* or the *boys* who hit the ball. Rarely do they risk using a sentence as complex and sexually neutral as, perhaps, "The ball hit the side of the house and broke a window." They also rarely use collective pronouns — the children, the club, friends, the class or they, us or we. But when they do use words less clearly descriptive of the sex of the actors — for example, "The children are going on a hike." — they quickly dispel any possibility that "children" might include girls by providing a picture of five little boys and their male leader. So, through the use of highly specific words and pictures the dictionaries used by the youngest — and most impressionable — children are the most effective at rendering females invisible.

Of all the picture dictionaries on the market (and on library and preschool classroom shelves) Richard Scarry's *Best Word Book Ever* (Hamlyn 1970) is probably the most blatant example of this phenomenon of erasing a significant part of the population. Since Scarry's sales have exceeded the million mark (he has made the *New York Times* Index of the ten best-selling children's books), I assume he is also erasing many of his young readers.

By using humorous animals to help define words, he does avoid the insidious racism of most of the other books which consistently show Anglo-Saxon looking people and use Anglo-Saxon names. But he does make it very possible for us to tell which animals are male and which are female. The few females that do turn up in his pages are clearly labelled with aprons, ribbons and skirts. They are found in the following numbers in these sections:

At the Playground	32 boys	11 girls
Using Tools	10 boys	0 girls
Toys	14 boys	2 girls
Boats and Ships	13 boys	0 girls
Making Music	24 boys	2 girls
Making Things Grow	4 boys	0 girls
At the Airport	11 boys	1 girl

And on and on and on. Others might come up with slightly different counts since some animals have no clothes or are very small. I won't quibble since the ratios are still very dramatic. The lexicographer's computer found that "overall the ratio in schoolbooks of *he* to *she, him* to *her* was almost 4 to 1". Scarry usually does much worse than that.

The *Best Word Book Ever* can certainly leave its young readers wondering just what little girls and women do do. Well, in *When You Grow Up* Scarry shows us that females can be secretaries, singers, teachers, dancers, librarians and mummies; in *Health,* he shows us a nurse and a dental hygienist. So girls can have jobs, but they don't do much playing, planting, making things or going places. In *Things We Do,* while 32 male animals are pursuing a whole host of life-sustaining activities (riding bikes, driving cars, planting and selling food), the two females on the pages are used to illustrate the activities "sitting" and "watching".

While the picture dictionaries are blatantly sexist, the more sophisticated ones for older readers show a similar myopia. In reading the definition of "professional", I was shocked to find the helpful sentence, "A lawyer or a doctor is a professional man." Obviously, the remote possibility that a lawyer or a doctor might be a professional *woman* never crossed the editor's mind. Yet the sentence would have read well and been sexually neutral by the simple omission of the last word in the sentence.

The dictionaries for older children also show few illustrations of females. If they're illustrating how one plays an accordion or uses a compass, if they're showing the position of the alimentary canal in the human body or a facial

expression, most pictures show male figures — unless the task
or object is unequivocally or stereotypically linked with
women like an item of clothing or a domestic, especially
childcaring, activity.

This leads us to our third, not very surprising, conclusion.

**3. When female pronouns, names or pictures are used, they
help define or illustrate the most intransitive, passive verbs
and the most negative or subordinate nouns and adjectives.**

The Golden Dictionary (Hamlyn 1966), a best-selling classic
like the *Best Word Book Ever,* helped me quickly identify this
pattern. I needed only to look at its first page, where I found:

Able: John is *able* to touch his toes.

Ann is *not able* to touch her toes.
At: John is *at* the top of the ladder.

Ethel is *at* the bottom (actually on the ground, according
to the illustration).
Asleep: Jenny is *asleep.*
Awake: Bob is *awake.*

Lest I too quickly generalise, however, I decided to explore
systematically the active-male, passive-female bias I suspected
existed in all the books. I listed several often-used verbs,
nouns and adjectives and then looked them up in the
dictionaries. Here is a sampling of what I found (in some
instances the word was not defined in every dictionary or it
was not used in a sentence or was not sex-linked). The active
verbs were always linked to makes.

Lead: The *man leads* the horse.

I will *lead* my pony through the door. [picture of a
boy]
He leads the horses to water.
He always takes the *lead* when we plan to do
something.
Bob wanted to *lead.*
He plays the *lead* in the school play.
Fix: Patsy broke her doll. *Father fixed* it.

I broke my toy. *Daddy* will *fix* it. [picture of a girl]
The man *fixed* the post into the ground.
See *father fix* the tree.
Jim fixed the tent stakes firmly in the ground.

More passive verbs were represented by collective pronouns, animals or females.

Sit: I sit in a chair. [picture of both a boy and a girl].
    The *dog,* Chips, can *sit* up and ask for food.
    The *woman sat* the little boy down hard.
Lay: Ruth lay her doll in the cradle.
    See *mother lay* the baby on the bed.
    Ma laid the baby in the cradle.
    She lay down when she was tired.

In the few instances in which active verbs were linked to a female pronoun, they were often used in the most passive, trivial or negative way. For example.

Tom swims in the water.
James swam to the other side of the pool.
Most *boys* like to *swim.*
He swam the river.

But "*Her* eyes were *swimming* with tears." While *Father* was *fixing* broken toys, *"Mother fixed* 6:00 as dinner hour" and *"Regina fixed* her collar". While the *boys were hitting* the ball with a bat or racket, "the *girls hit* upon a good name for their club." While *he threw* himself at his opponent, *"she threw* a cape over her shoulders."

When I looked up definitions of nouns and adjectives, ...I found those with great social prestige were almost uniformly male. For example,

Brave: Jim was *brave* in the dentist's chair.
    The *soldiers braved* much danger.
    He *braved* the king's anger.

The *soldier* was *brave*.

The *men braved* the blizzard.

Wise: My *father* is a *wise* man.

The three *wise men* came from the east to honour the baby Jesus.

The *man* is very *wise*.

Wise men.

A *wise* states*man*.

Those words with less social prestige were associated with animals or females or were not sex-linked.

Afraid: The *cat* is *afraid* of the dog.

The *cat* is *afraid* to jump.

Alice is *afraid* of snakes.

Cat is *afraid* of the dog.

Jane is *afraid* of spiders.

Wrong: Mrs. Brown is doing her child a *wrong* by spoiling him.

Mary spelled three words *wrong*.

Tom *rarely* does the *wrong* thing.

He's not wrong.

Purple is the *wrong* colour for *her*.

They *wronged her* by telling lies.

Mixed-up: The children *mix* their *mother up* when they ask her to do so many things at once. She doesn't know what she is doing.

4. While the stereotyping in children's dictionaries is pervasive, there are some hopeful signs of publishers' awareness of the issues.

Of the books I reviewed, the *Xerox Intermediate Dictionary* (published in 1973) and *The American Heritage School Dictionary* (published in 1972) appear to be substantial improvements over their outdated but still much-in-use predecessors. Though it looks quite modern and liberated at first glance, the *Xerox Dictionary* is still probably not worth buying. On closer reading I found it cautious and non-committal to a fault. While it avoids negatively stereotyping

women in many definitions, it also rarely positively affirms
female strength, nor, for that matter, does it affirm male
warmth and vulnerability. I found little evidence that it has
taken note of the civil rights movement or other recent
political or social developments. It simply screens out
blatantly stereotyped allusions by avoiding sex linking and
continues to repeat worn-out male-oriented phrases.

The American Heritage Dictionary, while still skewed in the
direction of male and Anglo-Saxon dominance, does confront
sterotyping in several instances. It not only avoids
perpetuating stereotypes but deliberately overthrows several.
For example, while the very inadequate *Webster's New World
Dictionary for Young Readers* (supposedly revised in 1971)
defines:

Prostitute: "A person who does immoral things for money,
especially a woman who offers herself to men for money."

and *Xerox* avoids the issue by not listing the word, the
American Heritage defines:

Prostitute: "Someone who debases himself or his abilities for
money or an unworthy motive. Someone who performs sexual
acts for pay."

Clearly, thought was given to the latter definition; it more
adequately mirrors reality, and explains the term. *The
American Heritage* declares itself to be the first dictionary to
list and define the title Ms. (although it doesn't feel ready to
confirm how to pronounce it). Although it is the only
dictionary I read that listed NAACP, it did not, regrettably,
do more than explain what the initials stood for. It mentions
student anti-war protests in one of its definitions and offers a
very dignified description of the suffragette Amelia Bloomer,
who is often not credited with the seriousness of purpose she
deserves. In providing phrases for the word proud, it quite
appropriately uses the phrase "black pride".

In its choice of illustrations, *The American Heritage*

Dictionary has made an obvious effort to include more females, and in some instances, it shows Third World youngsters. A photograph of two black girls illustrates the game of "leap frog", while an Asian girl shows us how to play the "triangle".

The comparison of these two shiny new books leads me to my final conclusion.

5. Since you can't tell how stereotyped a dictionary is by its sales totals, fancy cover or date of revision, you must check for yourself each dictionary you find on the school, library or bookshop shelf.

It's a good idea to develop a few tests to "check out" a dictionary. First you might list five active and five passive words, five negative and five positive ones, and see how the book defines them both in words and pictures. Then look up traditionally stereotyped words like gossip, tattle, tease, leader, courage and determination to see how they are handled. Check your favourite sport or hobby and see who is defined or shown pursuing it. See how often they use man and mankind rather than people or humans. Flip through the illustrations and see who is shown using the compass and who is shown using the typewriter.

When you find a dictionary that lists the term cavepeople and shows a sketch of a Neanderthal woman, uses George Washington in a sentence to show the word "slave holder" in context, shows a female demonstrating how a microscope is used, and routinely avoids he, his and him by using plural nouns and pronouns, buy a copy for yourself and pass the news on to several teachers and librarians.

A Guide to Sex Education Books

Dick Active, Jane Passive

Joan Scherer Brewer

Motivated by anthropological, biological, and psychological research, and influenced by modern technology, authors now writing about human sexual behaviour crowd adult book lists with such provocative titles as Merlin Stone's *Paradise Papers* (Virago 1976) and John Money and Patricia Tucker's *Sexual Signatures* (Abacus 1977). These books question the necessity to conform to traditional masculine and feminine stereotypes and present visions of a liberated age when a broad spectrum of sexual behaviour will be "acceptable", an age when biological sex will no longer define one's expression of sexual feelings. Life styles discussed ranged from the traditional nuclear family to group marriage, "open" marriage, same-sex marriage, and to remaining unmarried with or without children.

But are these new insights and more open attitudes reflected in the sex education books being read by the future adults of this supposedly liberated culture? It would seem not. I have surveyed titles recommended for young children by public and school librarians in my middle-sized community — a community that is a mixture of agrarian, industrial, business, and intellectual micro-societies — and I have given specific attention to those titles that have wide circulation. I have also studied some of the books in the library of the Institute for Sex Research. Most of the books cited here also appear on the standard recommended book lists and catalogues of sex education materials.

What the CIBC has found to be true in other areas of children's literature is also true in the sex education field. Sexist stereotypes abound, and racism is implicit in the absence of characters other than whites in illustrations. Life styles other than those of traditional middle-class, white heterosexuals are disparaged either explicitly or by omission.

Socially determined differences between the sexes are described as if they were biologically determined. Anti-humanistic values are projected, especially in books for teenagers. Despite assurances that everyone is different and that "popularity" is not the honest measure of personal worth, emphasis is, at the same time, given to how to attract the opposite sex through successful role playing.

Disservice is done to girls at every socio-economic level by conveying the impression that a female's essential worth resides in her ability to become a mother. In most of these sex education books, women are portrayed only as wives and mothers realising their reproductive potential. Women are not shown as humans first who possess, among other attributes, the ability to conceive and reproduce life. As in other children's literature, doctors are all men; nurses, women. Female sexuality is presented as mainly passive — females are receptacles for sperm. In their otherwise excellent *How Babies Are Made* (Time-Life, 1969) Andrew C. Andry and Steven Schepp write: "the father places his penis in the mother's vagina," a one-sided definition that recurs slightly paraphrased in book after book. Boys and men are most often described in terms of their biological destiny as sperm producers and husbands-fathers-providers, and as solely responsible for the active element of coitus.

Rarely is the coital act seen as a source of pleasure, but in some exceptional books it is. Per Holm Knudsen in his delightful *How a Baby is Made* (Franklin Watts 1973, Piccolo 1975) observes that during sexual intercourse the father and mother "hold each other tightly, and move together happily". In Sol Gordon's *Girls Are Girls and Boys Are Boys* (Day, 1974), the reader learns that "Most of the time people have sexual intercourse because it feels good, and not because they want to have a baby.''

Heterosexuality is assumed to be universal and the norm by most sex education authors writing for the preschool-primary groups. When mentioned in the intermediate books, discussions of homosexuality warn about social stigma or rapacious adults who might try to seduce unwary youths because ''they are sick or very unhappy''. Although a certain amount of same-sex experimentation is granted as being a natural, passing phase, the continuation of close relationships with friends of the same sex is often portrayed as tempting fate and a reason to seek ''help''. Only Wardell Pomeroy's books and *Make It Happy* discuss bisexuality. *Any* degree of sexual attraction to the same sex is described as equivalent to a homosexual orientation.

Most sex education books, of course, introduce and explain male-female biological differences. They also include explanations of sexual behaviour that are functions of these differences, although a few books avoid any mention of any type of sex act, cloaking the act of conception in mystery and noting only that it results from a process called ''the love of married people''. Too often, however, while claiming to be doing no more than writing about biology, authors go on to include culturally determined maleness/masculinity, femaleness/femininity concepts in such a way that young readers can only deduce that anatomy is indeed destiny. Brief reviews of the books surveyed follow.

Andry, Andrew C. and Steven Schepp. Illustrated by Blake Hampton. **How Babies Are Made.** Time-Life, London, 1969.

The illustrations are all done with paper sculpture. The first and last pictures are of five children, each with different skin tones and racial characteristics. Other illustrations are of animals or white humans. The central characters illustrating conception and birth are white.

Sexuality is discussed only in the context of procreation,

137

and the terms "mother" and "father" are used instead of male and female for all life forms pictured, animal or human.

Intercourse is defined explicitly, but with the usual image of the passive female: "father places his penis in the mother's vagina... they are sharing a very personal and special relationship." The mother and father are shown in bed, kissing, covered by blankets up to their bare shoulders. The mother is smiling and the picture suggests an element of pleasure in the act of conception.

The final part of the text emphasises the equal role of the male and female in the creation of new life, and the story is about how babies grow rather than being a polemic to motivate the reader to become a parent.

Gordon, Sol. Illustrated by Frank C. Smith. **Girls Are Girls and Boys Are Boys.** John Day, New York, 1974.

Director of the Institute for Family Relations and Education at Syracuse University, Gordon has written a number of innovative sex education books which attempt to serve the needs of all races and socio-economic levels. This book, subtitled "so what's the difference?", is a frontal attack on sex-role stereotyping. Through the illustrations, racism by omission is also combated. Illustrations show blacks and whites interacting in a variety of roles.

Physiological differences are explained, and intercourse is described in the context of procreation, but these factors are incidental to the primary message that there should be equal encouragement and opportunities for both sexes to choose whatever they wish as their adult goals. The possibility that some girls would rather grow up and be doctors than marry and be mothers, or be a number of things at once, is introduced.

This is the only book on this reading level to mention masturbation ("an enjoyable feeling for both boys and girls") and birth control ("Most of the time people have sexual intercourse because it feels good, and not because they want to have a baby. So they use birth control...").

It is such an excellent effort I hesitate to complain, but once more the image of the male as the active participant in intercourse and conception is conveyed: "... if they want to have a child the man puts his penis into the woman's vagina and deposits his sperm."

Knudsen, Per Holm. **How a Baby is Made.** (Franklyn Watts 1973, Piccolo 1975).

This delightful picture book was first published in Denmark in 1971 and, in common with all Scandinavian productions reviewed here, the illustrations are stylised representations of white human characters.

In humorous (humour and sex!) illustrations, the true story is indeed told. The reader is shown the mother and father, who seem on a very equal basis, completely nude and embracing. The male's erection is pictured, and there is a full-length illustration of the partners holding "each other tightly" while they "move together happily", with a cutaway view of how the penis fits into the vagina. This is something not even most secondary and adult texts bother to explain.

The pictures are deliberately stylised and humorous to remove them a step from reality and to make the clinical details incidental to the story. The objective is to have a child accept the book as just another enjoyable picture book while absorbing the information almost unconsciously.

One would hope that this attractive and charming book, which explains sex and procreation accurately, frankly, unmysteriously and unromantically, will gain a large readership. I am buying copies as gifts for new-born babies.

Sheffield, Margaret. Illustrated by Sheila Bewley. **Where Do Babies Come From?** Cape 1972.

First published in London in 1972, this book was featured in the May, 1973, issue of *Ms.* magazine as one of their "Stories for Free Children" in connection with an article criticising sexism in sex education books.

The characters in the illustrations are unidentifiable by race but are not Anglo-Saxon or Nordic types. Males and females are pictured with equal lyricism. The birth scene shows natural childbirth with the mother being assisted by an attendant who could be a woman, instead of the usual male doctor.

In showing the difference between the sexes, a nude girl is pictured with the text "Young girls have a womb and a vagina..." In another illustration there is a baby girl and the text reads "This is a girl baby. She has a vagina." In both instances the vulva is shown, a common practice in every book at this reading level.

Intercourse is illustrated by a waist-up picture of a nude man and woman lying down and embracing. The text reads, "This is how babies are begun, with the man lying so close to the woman that his penis can fit into her vagina." Both illustration and text make male and female equally passive, which is at least a step toward equalising responsibility.

The book focuses on the processes of conception and birth, emphasising the equal role men and women play without making a case for everyone in the world becoming mothers and fathers.

Mayle, Peter. **Where Did I Come From?** Macmillan 1978.

Witty cartoons drawn by Arthur Robins give this book a cheerful charm. Intercourse is described in detail, (orgasm is a "tremendously big lovely shiver"). The sexual act, as illustrated by a rollicking couple, looks both enjoyable and friendly. The birth of a baby is covered but, sadly, not shown. (Ed.)

Pomeroy, Wardell B. **Boys and Sex.** Pelican 1970.
Pomeroy, Wardell B. **Girls and Sex.** Pelican 1971.

The author draws on his experience as a researcher with Dr. Alfred Kinsey and as co-author of *Sexual Behaviour in the Human Male* and *Sexual Behaviour in the Human Female* in writing these two volumes popular among young teenagers. Although one must question whether some of the female characteristics described are due to culturally-induced role playing rather than to biology ("Girls... think... in terms of dating... the boy is sexually excited..."), on the whole the author strives for a non-sexist approach. The focus is on real adolescent concerns of dating, petting and premarital sex. Masturbation and homosexuality are explained as variations in sex behaviour. Homosexuality is seen as a problem mainly because our society and our laws make it so.

Widerberg, Siv; translated from Swedish by Irene D. Morris. Illustrated by Michael Grimsdale. **The Kids' Own XYZ of Love and Sex.** Neville Spearman 1972.

This book was first published in Sweden in 1971 as *Mamma, Pappa, Barn.* The author challenges sex-role stereotypes from the beginning. Information is conveyed through a conversation between a little girl and her father, who is preparing lunch for mother and brothers. The only difference between the sexes is that a male has male sex organs, a female has female organs — in sexual feelings and behaviour, they are equals. All variations of heterosexual relations are discussed as all right between consenting persons. The girl asks, and is told how people get to be single parents. Homosexuality, however, is not mentioned.

Mayle, Peter. **What's happening to Me?** Macmillan 1978.

Aimed at 10-14 year olds "suffering from growing pains" this book supplies some of the facts that **Where Did I Come From?** left out, although there's no mention of homosexuality and the large format, so suitable for younger children, might well be scorned by older readers. (Ed.)

Cousins, Jane. **Make it Happy.** Virago 1978.

A very full account of all aspects of sex. Stereotyping of

males and females is discussed, as are homosexuality and bisexuality. The tone is, as the book claims, "honest, frank and reassuring". (Ed.)

How To Look for Racism and Sexism in Children's Books: A Guideline

1 Check the Illustrations

a) Look for stereotypes: happy-go-lucky banana-eating Black Sambos, inscrutable slant-eyed yellow orientals, the cottage-loaf mother, the demure doll-loving daughter.

b) Look for tokenism: if there are non-white characters shown, do they look like whites except for their tint or colour? Do all minority-group faces look the same — or are they depicted as genuine individuals?

c) Who's doing what? Are black or brown characters, or females, shown in leadership and action roles?

2 Check the Storyline

a) Standards for success: is success in the white-dominated society projected as the only ideal? Does a black person have to have outstanding qualities to be accepted? In friendships between white and non-white characters is it the non-white who does most of the understanding and forgiving?

b) Resolution of problems: are minority people treated as "the problem"? Are the reasons for poverty explained, or accepted as inevitable? Is a particular problem faced by a minority person resolved only through benevolent white intervention?

c) Role of women. Are female achievements due only to good looks? Could the same story be told if the sex roles were reversed?

3 Look at the Lifestyles

Are minority people and their setting unfavourably contrasted with the unstated norm of white middle-class suburbia? If the illustrations and text attempt to depict another culture, do they go beyond over-simplifications to offer genuine insights into another lifestyle? Look for inaccuracy and inappropriateness in the depiction of other cultures.

4 Watch Relationships

Do the whites in the story possess the power, take the leadership, and make the important decisions? Do non-whites and females function in essentially supporting roles?

How are family relationships depicted? In black families, is the mother always dominant? If the family are separated, are social conditions — unemployment, poverty — among the reasons for the separation?

5 Heroes and Heroines

When minority heroes and heroines do appear, are they admired for the same qualities that have made their white counterparts famous or because what they have done has benefited white people? Whose interests is a particular figure really serving?

6 Consider the Effects on a Child

Does the book counteract or reinforce a positive association with the colour white and a negative with black?

What happens to a girl's self-esteem when she reads that boys perform all the brave and important deeds?

In a particular story, is there anyone with whom a minority child can readily and positively identify?

7 Check the Author's Perspective

No author can be wholly objective. All authors write out of a cultural as well as a personal context. Look carefully to see whether the direction of the author's perspective weakens or strengthens the value of her written work.

8 Watch for Loaded Words

Examples of loaded adjectives (usually racist) are *savage, primitive, inscrutable,* and *backward.*

Look for sexist language, and adjectives that exclude or ridicule women: look for the use of the male pronoun to refer to both males and females. The following examples show how sexist language can be avoided: *ancestors* instead of *forefathers, community* instead of *brotherhood, manufactured* instead of *man-made.*

9 Look for the Copyright Date

Books on minority themes — usually hastily conceived — suddenly began appearing in the mid-1970s. There followed a growing number of "minority experience" books to meet the new market demand, but most of these were still written by white authors, edited by white editors and published by white publishers. They therefore reflected a white point of view. Only very recently has the children's book world begun even remotely to reflect the realities of a multiracial society. And it has only just begun to reflect feminist concerns.

The copyright dates, therefore, can be a clue as to how likely the book is to be overtly racist or sexist, although a recent copyright date, of course, is no guarantee of a book's relevance or sensitivity.

Contributors

RAE ALEXANDER, a graduate of Bank Street College of Education, is a graduate in reading and sociolinguistics. She is co-author with Julius Lester of *What it's like to be Young and Black in America* (Random House).

LOIS KALK BOUCHARD is a freelance writer and author of *The Boy who Wouldn't Talk* (Doubleday).

JOAN SCHERER BREWER is reference librarian at the Institute for Sex Research at Indiana University. She holds degrees from Syracuse and Indiana Universities.

MARY CADOGAN and PATRICIA CRAIG are co-authors of *You're a Brick, Angela!* (A new look at girls' fiction from 1839 to 1975) published by Gollancz in 1976.

ARIEL DORFMAN is a Chilean literary critic and novelist. Before the Pinochet Coup he was Professor of Spanish American Literature at the University of Chile. He now lives in exile.

JANET HILL, a former children's librarian, is Assistant Director of Lambeth Amenity Services (Libraries).

SHARON BELL MATHIS, a graduate in library science, is author of several children's books.

ARMAND MATTELART is a sociologist who was Professor of Mass Communications at the University of Chile before the coup. He has written several books and made a feature length film on Chile.

KIK REEDER is a Swedish writer-journalist who has been working for the Scandinavian Press as fiction editor.

BARBARA A. SCHRAM is co-ordinator of the Human Services Programme in the School of Education, Northeastern University, and consultant to Bank Street College of Education's Day Care Unit. She has worked as community organiser for welfare rights and community participation in schools, and is active in several feminist groups.

DR ALBERT V. SCHWARTZ is Associate Professor of Education at the City University of New York.

CARLA STEVENS, formerly children's book editor at Young Scott Books, is an instructor at the New School for Social Research, and author of several children's books.

JUDITH STINTON is a freelance writer and editor. She has worked in a number of city bookshops where she was responsible for children's books, and also in the children's section of an Inner London public library.

ISABELLE SUHL, specialist in library work with children, is librarian of Elisabeth Irwin High School in New York City.

BINNIE TATE was formerly children's librarian at Los Angeles Public Library and has taught black courses at the Universities of Wisconsin, Milwaukee, and California State College.